Praise for Inflection Point

"**Traci Medford-Rosow's** book, *Inflection Point*, is a captivating memoir, reflecting the personal and poignant side of a multi-billion dollar corporate struggle over the drug, Lipitor®. Often times, readers can get so bogged down with the convoluted wrangling and parsing involved in legal cases that a story can lose its personal connection to the reader. Not the case with *Inflection Point!*

Well-written and informative, I appreciated the personal nature of Traci's storytelling, from the psychedelic pants to her involvement in the international intellectual property battle, from the individual lives of Traci and colleagues to insights and to defining Court Decisions, I felt a personal connection to the author and her intriguing story. Sometimes we don't pay enough attention to the human side of headline stories and news reports. An incredible read!" — **Laura Ponticello**, Divine Phoenix Books

"A compelling narrative of the author's personal journey leading the biggest patent battle in history."— **Joe O'Malley**, Global Head of the intellectual property group at Paul Hastings LLP

"An incredible memoir that is an inherently fascinating read, *Inflection Point* provides a rare insider's look at an aspect of the pharmaceutical industry that is seldom revealed to the public. Exceptionally well written, organized and presented, *Inflection Point* deserves as wide a readership as possible as the issues of public health and the role played by 'big pharmacy' is under increasing controversy and political scrutiny. Simply stated, *Inflection Point* needs to be a part of every community and academic library collection for the benefit of non-specialist general readers and academia alike." — **Midwest Book Review**

"*Inflection Point* is a business story, a pharmaceutical story, a sociological story, and a personal, emotional story. (**Traci Medford-Rosow**) keeps the story moving at a quick pace with a good writing style that keeps the reader interested...(a) sobering read into a world few know much about." — **San Francisco Book Review**

What Amazon readers are saying:

"…a richly textured and rare glimpse into the legal battle for intellectual property rights…"

"The heart of the story is transformation. The courage and tenacity to stand in one's own truth…"

"I actually couldn't put this book down!"

Exciting, "Non-Generic" Account Of Saving Lipitor®.

"When I think of lawyerly writing, I don't necessarily think of writing that moves me. Henceforths, herewiths and theretos may serve a high and noble purpose, but they aren't exactly evocative. But **Medford-Rosow's** writing is evocative and so is her story.

Her heart is big. Just how big is immediately apparent from the book's early version of herself as a protective older sister. And it's a heart that never shrinks as the youthful competitive swimmer she was in Virginia travels to Manhattan and evolves as a big fish in the giant pond of Big Pharma. It's the heyday of Lipitor and she heads up IP at drug giant Pfizer.

The bulk of the book's legal drama focuses on an epic threat to Lipitor's patent that chews up years of her legal wits, attention and energy. It's exciting stuff and makes for engaging reading. That's because **Medford-Rosow's** story cleverly doubles the meaning of IP to not only represent the standard "Intellectual Property", as in Pfizer's gold-plated statin, but to also stand for *Inflection Point*, her personal navigation through the corporate pressure cooker as the pill maker becomes pill crusher and she must get out or risk being ground to powder. If you think only blue-collar types suffer from work-related injuries, read the chronicling of her physical battle wounds as her white collar pressures intensify and try not to make a comparison to other types of workplace maladies (I thought of coal workers' black lung disease and the knocked out teeth of hockey players).

Questioning her fortitude as the legal battle lumbers on, the author looks back in time, back to Virginia, back to her childhood homestead to see exactly how she got where she is and what it is that makes her stay. She addresses a surprising history found nowhere on her corporate CV and in doing so changes her present and the course of her future.

A storyline in the book involving the author's associate, Carol, that I won't spoil by revealing here, is so remarkably positive, it made me want to run out and pay something forward, do some good. Maybe I watched too many seasons of Glenn Close playing the nasty lawyer in *Damages*, but it was an eye-opener to read about anyone, lawyers included, so full of encouragement for another human being.

I started reading Inflection Point late one night after I downloaded it on my iPad. I didn't know what to expect, my experience with pharmaceutical employees is primarily drug reps with John Edwards haircuts and shiny shoes. But it had me, right from when I first double-clicked it and I didn't darken my screen until the book was done. I can't remember the last time that happened."

Powerful and Inspiring

"**Traci Medford-Rosow's** memoir provides the reader a richly textured and rare glimpse into the legal battle for the intellectual property rights of the drug Lipitor, while employed as Chief Intellectual Property Counsel, for one of the largest pharmaceutical companies in America (Pfizer). At core, Inflection Point is a pyscho-social narrative about the personal and professional challenges, setbacks and triumphs the author experienced during the litigation process, and as captivating, her keen insight into life itself. **Medford-Rosow** artfully infuses the nodal "points" in time that changed Pfizer's trajectory and with candor and self-reflection painfully depicts her own "points" of emotional transcendence. At times, with the weight of the world seemingly on her shoulders, the author is battle tested in all aspects of life and has the psychological scars to prove it. Nevertheless, her fearless nature shines brilliantly. Like a lighthouse at sea she is a "point"—a beacon of hope—and an illustration of tenacious courage for each of us as we encounter the difficulties inherent in work, life, and love. A wonderful read for those interested in legal issues in the corporate sector; a must read for those individuals who appreciate the changing nature of the human condition and the possibility of turning points."

Inflection Point

War and Sacrifice in
Corporate America

Traci Medford-Rosow

PEGASUS BOOKS

Pegasus Books
3338 San Marino Ave
San Jose, CA 95127
www.pegasusbooks.net

First Edition: December 2015

Published in North America by Pegasus Books. For information, please contact Pegasus Books c/o Christopher Moebs, 3338 San Marino Ave, San Jose, CA 95127.

This book is a work of non-fiction. Some names have been changed to protect the privacy of individuals.

Library of Congress Cataloguing-In-Publication Data
Traci Medford-Rosow
Inflection Point/Traci Medford-Rosow– 1st ed
p. cm.
Library of Congress Control Number: 2015956242
ISBN – 978-1-941859-42-1

1. BUSINESS & ECONOMICS / Industries / Pharmaceutical & Biotechnology.
2. LAW / Intellectual Property / Patent. 3. BUSINESS & ECONOMICS /
Corporate & Business History. 4. MEDICAL / Pharmacy. 5. BIOGRAPHY &
AUTOBIOGRAPHY / Personal Memoirs. 6. LAW / Ethics & Professional
Responsibility.

10 9 8 7 6 5 4 3 2 1

Comments about *Inflection Point* and requests for additional copies, book club rates and author speaking appearances may be addressed to Traci Medford-Rosow or Pegasus Books c/o Christopher Moebs, 3338 San Marino Ave, San Jose, CA, 95127, or you can send your comments and requests via e-mail to cmoebs@pegasusbooks.net.

Also available as an eBook from Internet retailers and from Pegasus Books

Printed in the United States of America

For JAT—All is forgiven.

ACKNOWLEDGEMENTS

First, I would like to thank my brother, Jeff Medford, for agreeing to tell the part of this story that is linked to our mother. To Marcus McGee and Chris Moebs from Pegasus, thank you for taking a chance on this book and for your patience during its completion. Many thanks to my two amazing editors, Richard Kelley, who taught me to write, and Peter Skutches, who completely understood the story I was trying to tell and why. A heartfelt thanks to Rhonda Turner, who believed in the project from the first early draft and led me to my steadfast agent, Sam Fleishman. Much gratitude to my law partner, Peter Richardson, who read an untold number of drafts, and to my husband, Joel Rosow, who encouraged me to never give up on my goal of telling this story to the fullest extent possible. I would also like to thank Nancy Perry Graham, Bill Looney, Joe O'Malley, Lynne Mitchell, Torey Via Worron, Jeff Worron, Grace Medford, Jesse Kornbluth, and my daughter, Kyra Rosow, who all read drafts at different stages of the book's development and offered me their honest and candid assessment, invariably pointing me in directions I had not yet considered exploring. And, finally, a special thanks to my son, Chad Rosow, who came up with the book's title.

War and Sacrifice in Corporate America

Replete with intrigue, *Inflection Point* is the true story of the author and her legal team at Pfizer who found themselves at the epicenter of the decade long, world-wide, multi-billion dollar battle for control over the world's most prescribed pharmaceutical product, Lipitor®. The author charts the course of the team's courageous effort to protect the company's most prized asset, and the unforeseen personal consequences suffered as a result.

In New York, London, Paris, Copenhagen, and Ottawa, from the White House to Wall Street, in boardrooms and courtrooms, in the media and behind closed doors, critical disputes are won and lost in a struggle for survival.

Inflection Point is a fast-paced, high-stakes legal thriller and memoir. But it is also a cautionary tale posing a question as fundamental as it is critical: Have the efforts to bring affordable medicines to consumers helped to cripple the very industry that invents life-saving drugs in the first place?

INFLECTION POINT

Author's Note to Readers:

All events in this story are true. All the characters are real people except Will and Charlotte, who, for privacy concerns, are composites. Dr. Howard is a real person, but I have used his first name to protect his privacy, as well. Lipitor is Pfizer's registered trademark for atorvastatin calcium. According to Wikipedia, "Lipitor became the world's best-selling drug of all time, with more than US$125 billion in sales over approximately 14.5 years."

I have told the stories of the different Lipitor cases around the world in general terms. However, for those readers interested in more details, I have compiled key excerpts from the various decisions that can be found in the appendix.

Timeline of Key Events:

2003, January—Ranbaxy challenges Pfizer's Lipitor patents.
2003, February—Pfizer sues Ranbaxy in the U.S.
2004, December—U.S. trial.
2005, July—U.K. trial.
2005, October—U.K. trial decision.
2005, December—U.S. trial decision.
2006, July—Pfizer CEO Hank McKinnell is suddenly replaced by CEO Jeff Kindler.
2006, August—U.S. appellate decision; U.K. appellate hearing and decision.
2007, January—Canadian trial decision.
2007, July—Canadian appellate hearing.
2008, March—Canadian appellate decision.
2008, June—Worldwide Lipitor settlement agreement entered into between Pfizer and Ranbaxy.
2010, August—Author leaves Pfizer.
2010, December—CEO Jeff Kindler is replaced by Ian Read.
2011, November—Lipitor goes off-patent; the first of the antitrust lawsuits are filed against Pfizer and Ranbaxy over the Lipitor settlement.
2012, June—Supreme Court decision on Obamacare.
2013, June—Supreme Court decision on pay-for-delay provisions in patent settlements.

Inflection Point:

An event that results in a significant
change in the progress of a
company, industry, sector, or economy.

—Investopedia

My father is a feller of trees,

Or maybe just a gardener with a green thumb.

Picking the freshest wood to fiddle back, finger joint, gouge,

grain and hinge together.

Our house is filled with an assortment of wood,

But my father never talks about his furniture.

He prefers to talk about God, considering meditation with the

Buddhist cab driver,

His Jewish star dangling around his neck,

Never quite deciding what he believes.

One day I asked my father what he listens to when he makes his

furniture.

He just shrugged and said, "I don't. I just pray."

So after years of speculation, I finally realized my father has it

right.

Because to pray is to love.

And to love is to fiddle back, finger joint, gouge, grain,

And finally,

To hinge together.

Kyra Rosow

2012

TABLE OF CONTENTS

Prologue – Psychedelic Pants 1

PART ONE: Battles and Struggles 7

Chapter 1 – Water Lessons.. 9

Chapter 2 – Guided Missile.. 12

Chapter 3 – The Battle Begins 18

Chapter 4 – International Conflict... 24

Chapter 5 – Yellow Eyes 28

Chapter 6 – Small Sacrifices 35

Chapter 7 – Simplify... 39

Chapter 8 – Trial... 44

Chapter 9 – A Long Journey 51

Chapter 10 – White Wigs And Bombs 56

PART TWO: Wins And Losses... 63

Chapter 11 – The British Invasion 65

Chapter 12 – D-Day... 69

Chapter 13 – Unexpected Losses...72

Chapter 14 – European Madness 77

Chapter 15 – A Brooklyn Tale 82

Chapter 16 – The Longest Winter 87

Chapter 17 – O Canada... 93

Chapter 18 – The Ides Of March.. 99

Chapter 19 – Lost Innocence 104

Chapter 20 – Wedding Rings 108

PART THREE: Endings And Beginnings 115

Chapter 21 – Settlement... 117

Chapter 22 – Descent Into Darkness 120

Chapter 23 – Here We Go Again................................. 128

Chapter 24 – Au Revoir...133

Chapter 25 – Many Masters....................................135

Chapter 26 – Hard Choices 142

Chapter 27 – Dirty Laundry.................................... 146

Chapter 28 – End Of An Era.................................... 150

Chapter 29 – Viva Obamacare! 153

Chapter 30 – Sharp Edges.................................... 159

Chapter 31 – A Supreme Mess 162

Epilogue 168

Author's Final Note to Readers....................................172

COURT DECISIONS...177

Excerpts from Judge Farnan's Decision........................... 179

Excerpts from the CAFC Decision 195

Excerpts from Canadian Appellate Decision 198

Excerpts from U.K. Appellate Decision............................207

Excerpts from The Supreme Court Decision 213

PROLOGUE - PSYCHEDELIC PANTS
New York City, March 13, 2013

It was one of those things you know in your gut long before your brain can register what your eyes are seeing. At first, we both tried to explain it away, but before the day was over, the truth of what had happened to us was unimaginable, yet undeniable.

Peter Richardson, my law partner and long-term colleague and friend, and I were walking back to our office after lunch at one of our favorite little French bistros in midtown Manhattan when he called my attention to a young woman in front of us.

"Look at those pants!" he said.

It was, I think, the first time in the three decades we had been working together that he had called my attention to someone on the street—not that you could miss her. She looked like Lisbeth Salander, the title character in *The Girl with the Dragon Tattoo*, except, instead of black leather, nose rings, and tattoos, she was wearing the most outrageous pair of psychedelic pants I'd seen since the hippie '60s. They were neon-bright, a kaleidoscope of colliding colors: swirls of purple, yellow, red, and green striking a bold contrast to the gray overcast of the March sky.

Impossible to miss.

So the very last thing either of us thought at that moment was that she was a spy. Especially since she was in front of us rather than behind.

"Wow, those are bright," I replied. "But sort of a nice throwback."

Thinking nothing further of the woman or her pants, we continued on our way. Two blocks farther south, we stopped at the drug store to pick up a prescription. The normal ten-minute wait at the pharmacy ran a little longer than usual; a quarter hour later, back on Third Avenue, we were heading downtown to our office on East 37th Street.

And there she was again.

She'd evidently stopped to read her BlackBerry. I still didn't think too much of it then—I too have been known to stand on the street reading emails—but it was March, still winter, and still cold, and I remember that it crossed my mind that she must have been into one hell of an email exchange.

Now, late for an afternoon conference call, Peter and I hurried by the young woman in the psychedelic pants. Four blocks farther south, we turned right, and leaving behind the bustle of Third Avenue, we entered the quiet residential side street where our office was located in the commercial space of a Murray Hill townhouse.

We loved our little office and our two-man law firm. It was a totally different world from the one we'd spent in Big Pharma, each occupying those spacious corner offices with dazzling city views. But we were happy in the simplicity of our new world, with our few clients, and even with the extra responsibility that came with not having any assistants to help us with our daily work. Ours had become a small world, unhurried by corporate deadlines and unstressed by corporate bureaucracy.

Once inside our office, we realized that we'd left the case folder on the subject of our afternoon conference call in my apartment, a block away. So, less than a minute after we'd arrived, we were racing out of the office. And there she was, again, standing just a few feet past our door, to all appearances, still texting. My antennae went into full alert.

"Holy shit!" I exclaimed.

We both stopped dead in our tracks.

I looked at Peter; Peter looked at me.

I knew we were both thinking the same thing but were unable to comprehend that we were beholding that same pair of unusual psychedelic pants in the heart of midtown Manhattan for the third time in less than twenty minutes.

"Peter, what are the odds that she just happened to be standing outside the drug store when we left and now just happens to be standing outside our office?"

"Not very high. I think we're being followed," he replied with a sigh. "But, why?"

"I have no idea, but screw that! I'm going to follow her," I said and took off.

Her back was to me, but almost as if she had seen me coming after her, she started to run. She approached the corner when, without breaking stride, she turned her head around and looked at me. Our eyes locked for a split second. I was expecting her to turn left and continue south downtown when she abruptly turned right and headed back uptown in the same direction from which she'd just come, quickening her pace in the process. I followed suit.

At the next corner, she bolted across the street on the diagonal into four lanes of rapidly approaching traffic on Lexington Avenue, all the while looking at me over her shoulder. No sooner had she hit the sidewalk on the other side when she darted back across the street again, accelerating into a full-out sprint. Breathless, and with my mouth open, I stood on the sidewalk and watched her disappear. There was no way my old body could keep pace with a twenty-something year old.

After the shock wore off, I went to my apartment and called Peter.

"I'd like to think we are simply very popular, but there is only one explanation I can think of for us being followed," I said while relating the details of my further adventure.

"No doubt about it," he agreed with my unspoken conclusion. "And now we've blown our conference call to boot," Peter added, always the pragmatist between the two of us.

"Someone had to have been behind us feeding her information," I said, returning our conversation to the mysterious woman. "That is the only logical explanation for how she knew I'd taken off after her, and why she had turned her head around to look at me."

"Do you think this is the first time, or have we been followed before?" Peter asked, now clearly upset at what had become undeniable.

"No clue."

Peter and I were now retired from Pfizer. But we had both spent over thirty years working for the company in the legal division, and we'd been involved in a lot of high-profile litigation over the years, including the Lipitor patent infringement case and its settlement.

"And I'm guessing it's the same outfit that hacked into my computer," I said, remembering the unwelcome visitor I'd found scrolling through my *Inflection Point* files in the middle of the night the month before.

I'd been up late, unable to sleep, and had decided to pick off a few emails. Someone had suddenly taken over my computer, in much the same way a remote tech does when fixing it, and the cursor had started moving on its own. I had held my breath as my eyes had followed the cursor to the left side of my monitor, to my personal folders, where it had scrolled down until it had found my book's file. That was about as much intrusion as I had been able to manage. I'd started hitting the keyboard at random to make the intruder aware of my presence. In an instant, the control of the cursor had been returned to me, and the mysterious interloper had vanished into cyberspace. I'd wondered whether I had chased them off in time, however—before they'd found my secret folder. Their cursor had been close to it.

I couldn't be sure.

"It must have something to do with that Lipitor case," I repeated to Peter in suspended disbelief.

"I can't think of any other explanation," he agreed.

For the next few weeks we both felt uneasy. Was our office being bugged? Were we being watched and followed on a routine basis? We found ourselves looking under our desks and behind picture frames for the telltale signs of little cameras or microphones. We were unnerved when we noticed parked cars with casually waiting drivers outside our apartments, and for a period of time our otherwise ordinary life took on a cloak-and-dagger feel. We became agitated when we saw a strange, camera-like object hanging in the garden at the rear of the house next door to our office. It appeared to be pointed toward our windows. A few days later, it disappeared; we never learned what it was, who had put it there...or why.

Winter was at last giving way to the arrival of spring that end-of-March day when I sat at my desk, lost in thought. With the flowers came the first signs of new life, of hope, of a fresh beginning. I wondered whether I'd ever arrive at my own new beginning, if I'd ever get past the journey that had begun for me over a decade earlier on that cold, snowy January morning. I wondered whether the downward spiral of my life would ever reach the upward curve of the inflection point.

Here we go again...

PART ONE: BATTLES AND STRUGGLES

Courage is not the absence of fear,
but the triumph over it.
—Nelson Mandela

CHAPTER 1 – WATER LESSONS
Alexandria, Virginia, July 1967

Litigation is binary. You either win or you lose.

So is a swim race.

Unlike a group sport, you either win or lose on your own.

And everyone is watching.

I was only twelve years old when I learned one of the most important lessons of my life. A lesson that I would one day bring with me to New York City, to Corporate America, to the legal division of the world's largest pharmaceutical company.

But that summer, I was still a prepubescent young girl living in Virginia who escaped the summer heat, as well as the difficulties of her life, at the neighborhood swimming pool. As a seasoned competitive swimmer, I had already been stepping up on those starting blocks for six years, having competed in my first race as a six year old. So I was used to the pre-race jitters and had developed a split-second precision ability to take off the moment the start gun fired or, in a relay event, when my teammate's arm pulled out of the water for her final stroke. Even though my feet were not allowed to leave the starting block until her hand touched the wall, I knew by the time it took my brain to send the signal to my body to dive, her hand would be there.

On this particular morning, I was in an all-star relay event. The adrenaline was pumping through my bloodstream, and my brain cells were firing just a little bit faster than normal, making me trigger-happy. Or maybe it really wasn't the adrenaline after all. Maybe it was what had happened a few hours earlier in my bedroom during the fifteen minutes when my dad had left the house to buy the morning newspaper. Whatever the reason, three other girls depended on what I did. And what I did that morning was false start.

I knew it the instant I took off. Looking down, I could see my teammate's hand hit the wall a split second after my feet left the starting blocks. I knew a false start meant a disqualification even if my team won the race.

I hesitated in the water for half a moment as I weighed the odds—the odds that maybe the referee did not see that my feet had left the starting block early against the odds that if I turned around, swam back, and touched the wall again, my team would lose anyway. The race was already tight. My mind told me to just keep swimming—that the referee would not have seen my false start from her vantage point. But my gut was nagging me. Even at this young age, it was already a powerful force in my life.

Suddenly, I was swimming back down the pool in the wrong direction. I retagged the wall, flip-turned, and shot off in the right direction once again. I could see the other swimmers to my left and right, and they were all ahead of me. The lead I'd had when I'd started my lap was now blown. The only way to make up for the lost time was not to breathe, because each time you turn your face to take a breath, it slows down your pace a fraction of a second. So I turned my head to the side and took one last, giant breath of chlorine-filled summer air, put my face down in the water, and gave it everything I had.

I heard my father yelling his familiar "Pull, Traci" chant from the side of the pool. Inspired by his encouragement, I passed one swimmer after the next. The instant I hit the finish line, I jerked my head up and out of the water with the customary force. Only this time, I was not waiting for the timer to tell me the results of the race or looking over to find my father's smiling face or his thumb sticking straight up. I already knew our team had won.

This time I was looking up at the sky, mouth open, gasping for air.

As I pulled myself out of the water, my teammates were jumping up and down in excitement. I saw the referee approach. She positioned herself in front of me. My oxygen-starved brain was still disoriented, and I was sure she was going to tell me my team was disqualified even though I had retouched the wall. She placed her hand on my shoulder.

"It's a good thing you swam back and retagged the wall, young lady," she said. "I saw that false start of yours."

And so, I learned a valuable lesson that day in the pool. When my gut told me what to do in life, litigation, or especially in battle, I'd better not ignore it. And with very few exceptions, all of which I ended up regretting, I never did.

CHAPTER 2 - GUIDED MISSILE
New York City, January 2003

Like many ill-fated journeys, mine began with a late train. An icy wind blowing down the frozen train tracks whipped fresh snow around my face. I looked into my cup for the tiniest bit of warmth, but the coffee was already cold. Leaning past my fellow commuters and out over the edge of the station platform farther than was sensible, I looked impatiently for the arrival of the 7:04. The parallel rails merged into a vanishing point as the track disappeared into a vague, misty haze.

Nothing.

It was my first day back to the office after the holiday period, and I knew a lot of work would have accumulated on my desk during my short absence. I was anxious to get the day started.

As I continued to peer down the train track, I felt an uneasy sense of danger and foreboding that I brushed away along with the snowflakes on my eyelashes. One of my fellow commuters became alarmed.

"You're too close to the edge of the platform," she advised.

I took a few steps back and away from the platform's edge, an uncharacteristic show of caution on my part. And a tacit acknowledgement that she was right.

Several minutes later, the train arrived along with a swirl of snow that covered the recently shoveled platform. As we made our way south, I sat looking out the window at the pristine landscape. Even the city had a deceptively virgin freshness to it, blanketed in the newly-fallen snow. But despite the beauty, the short walk from Grand Central Station to my office at the corner of Lexington Avenue and 42nd Street proved to be a slippery challenge.

Bitter cold and late trains were going to be the least of the day's challenges, however. Before I returned home that evening, my team and I would be responsible for managing the biggest patent infringement case that the world's largest pharmaceutical company ever had to face. It would be a battle that would test every moral conviction I had, every truth I held self-evident, and every ounce of courage I possessed. It was a war that, in the end, would compromise my health, my mental stability, and my thirty-year career at Pfizer. I would master the art of making difficult sacrifices and overcoming the greatest of setbacks. But, most important of all, the decade-long journey I started that day would also teach me some of the most important lessons I would ever learn and to finally face a painful truth I had carefully hidden even from myself.

* * *

As I walked into my office my assistant jumped up from her desk and waved the morning mail at me.

"Please read this," she implored, following me and shutting the door behind us.

I took the letter she held out to me, but some of the pages dropped from my still frozen hands. My assistant bent down to pick them up. I squatted down as well, to help her shuffle the papers back into the correct order. Crouching together on the floor, facing each other, she caught my eye and held it. The urgency in her expression prompted me to read; it was clear she understood the significance of the letter she had just handed me. I looked down at the first page. One glance at the opening paragraph was enough. My breath caught in my throat. I found it difficult to stand back up.

Ranbaxy, a little-known generic company based in India, had just commenced a threat to Pfizer's best-selling product, Lipitor, the world's most popular cholesterol-fighting drug. Ranbaxy was challenging all the patents that protected it from generic competition and was seeking immediate approval to market its own copycat version. I tried to collect my thoughts. My assistant must have noticed my disconcertion.

"Traci, are you okay? Should I get you some coffee?"

"No, thanks. I'll go get it."

Still in my coat, I headed down to the cafeteria. Alone in the elevator, I started pacing in the enclosed space. How could this be? After twenty-five years at Pfizer, I had just taken over the job as head of global patent litigation. I'd known it would come with big responsibilities. But I could never have imagined this big.

* * *

Returning from the cafeteria, I picked up Ranbaxy's letter again and walked across the hall to Peter Richardson's office. It would be another eight years before we'd open our own law firm together and another decade before we'd be followed through the streets of New York City by the mysterious woman in psychedelic pants.

He was organizing the mail that had accumulated on his desk over the holidays, making a neat pile of the letters he wanted to keep and ditching the rest in the wastebasket—fastidious as always. He looked up when he saw me enter.

"Hey, good morning. How was your holiday?"

"Good until now," I replied, handing him Ranbaxy's letter.

"What's this?" he asked.

"Read for yourself."

A perplexed look spread across his normally serene face.

Lipitor was the biggest-selling pharmaceutical product of all time. The sales were already high and expected to grow as the headline on John Simon's *Fortune* magazine article made clear.

"The $10 Billion Pill: Hold the fries, please. Lipitor, the cholesterol-lowering drug, has become the bestselling pharmaceutical in history. Here's how Pfizer did it."

According to the Fortune article, "In 2002, Lipitor achieved estimated sales of $7.4 billion while commanding a 42% market share in this class of drugs, known as statins."

I was the head of global patent litigation. The responsibility for protecting Lipitor's patents lay in our group, referred to as the Intellectual Property Enforcement team. My brain sprung into high gear, despite the fact that I had not yet finished my morning coffee. Peter glanced up from Ranbaxy's letter, took off his glasses and rubbed his eyes. He looked tired, although it was not yet 9:00 a.m.

* * *

I returned to my office and called Jeff Kindler, Pfizer's general counsel. His assistant picked up.

"Can I speak to Jeff please?"

"He's not here, Traci."

"Please find him." I tried to keep the panic out of my voice.

"He's not here," she repeated. "Do you want to leave a voicemail?"

"Please find him," I repeated.

She got the message.

"Okay. I'll go find him."

Less than a minute later, he was on the phone. Even though he'd been with Pfizer for less than a year, he knew me well enough to understand that I wouldn't be calling so early without a pretty darn good reason. Kindler did not appreciate long-winded explanations—he was a busy man—and none was necessary that morning.

Kindler was one of the most charismatic men I'd ever met. He had captivated everyone at Pfizer from our board of directors on down. The first day I met him, I thought Pfizer was lucky to have lured him away from his previous employer—MacDonald's—as in the hamburger maker.

I was quick to share my thoughts with Peter.

"Wow, that guy is really great!"

"He sure is," Peter readily agreed.

Among his many skills, Kindler could work a room better than the ablest politician.

At one point during a large meeting, he was doing such a good job of it that one of my colleagues said under her breath, "What office is he running for?"

It proved to be a prescient comment. When, like a handsome senator, he focused his attention on you, you believed there was no one else in the room. And it felt good. With his perpetual tan, keen intelligence, and Harvard education, the package he presented to the company was that of a serious winner.

After concluding my call with Kindler, I sat back in my desk chair and waited for the inevitable call from Hank McKinnell, Pfizer's CEO. Hank was a serious type. Somewhat reserved and a bit aloof, he was nonetheless supportive of employees. He had started at Pfizer as a young man in 1971 and worked his way up the corporate ladder. Though some people found Hank cold, I never saw that side of his personality. I viewed him as the model of a CEO—one of Pfizer's best, brave and bold, and when he made a tough decision, he stuck to it. He was also a big fan of our legal team, often referring to us as his A-team and to me personally as his Crouching Tiger, Hidden Dragon. It proved to be a moniker more appropriate than McKinnell could have possibly imagined.

As I waited for the call from Hank, I gazed out the office window. Despite the scene below, the hustle and bustle of one of the busiest cities in the world, I felt an intense and unfamiliar loneliness. For the first time in my professional life, I was afraid. Even though I was not yet able to define the danger, I knew, without question, that it was real.

A dull, distant drum began to beat in my head. My life was about to change. I knew it at a cellular level, even though I tried to dismiss the mounting siren I heard in my ears.

But it was soon to reveal its true meaning.

A call to the battle that was about to begin.

CHAPTER 3 – THE BATTLE BEGINS
New York City, January 2003

Our team consisted of twenty people; all but three of us were legal professionals. We were known as the IPE team for short (another three letter acronym that had become quite common in those days), and we enjoyed a high profile within our Pfizer world.

Our job was to protect Pfizer's intellectual property. Because patent protection was critical to ensuring our company's continued survival, we were held in high esteem. We won cases no one else could. We were a magical group, each one of us a distinct individual, but together we composed a perfect symphony of talents and abilities. Best of all, we had each other and got along really well. We were like one large, extended family. I was the mother; Peter was our father. We all felt safe, and for a period of time, we lived in a magical kingdom all our own. Many of our colleagues noticed this.

"It is clear to me that you all actually like each other," Kindler said on more than one occasion, with a bit of awe and respect in his voice.

Our unity fascinated our observers at Pfizer. As might be expected at any large corporation, our magic aroused its quotient of jealousy from time to time, too.

* * *

Pfizer had just forty-five days to file a lawsuit against Ranbaxy in our effort to place a temporary stay on the approval of their proposed generic Lipitor product. If we failed to meet this deadline, then the Food and Drug Administration (FDA) could grant Ranbaxy's health approval, thus allowing its copycat product to enter the market.

Ranbaxy's challenge to Pfizer's Lipitor patents was made possible as a result of legislation, referred to as Hatch-Waxman (H-W). Passed by Congress in 1984, the act was intended to be a fair compromise between the research-based pharmaceutical companies that invent new drugs and the generic companies that copy them. A bit like communism, the deal looked great on paper but broke down over the years in practice. At first, the generics would typically challenge patents towards the end of the term of the drug's primary patents. But soon, generics began to challenge each and every patent as soon as was possible under the H-W rules. It seemed at times that, according to the generics, there was not a single valid pharmaceutical patent in the U.S.

In order to sell a pharmaceutical drug in the U.S., marketing approval must first be obtained from the FDA. This is a time-consuming and expensive process taking anywhere from ten to fifteen years and costing over a billion dollars. This daunting statistic is made even more so when one realizes that for every 10,000 new drugs discovered, only one ever makes it to market.

Prior to 1984, this onerous burden was required of generic drugs as well as branded ones. In an effort to get more lower-priced generic drugs to the American consumer, while maintaining incentives for innovation, Senator Orrin Hatch and Representative Henry Waxman negotiated a deal that allowed generic companies to piggy-back on data submitted to the FDA by the research-based company. As if this was not enough incentive for the generic companies, H-W added another sweetener to the deal. It awarded six months of marketing exclusivity to the first generic company to knock out a drug's patent, in essence awarding a mega million dollar prize (and in some cases a billion dollar one) to the generic company with the most aggressive and clever legal team. It didn't take the generics long before they were all trying to win this prize. and the law allowed generic companies to begin patent challenges just four short years after the name-brand product was launched.

One of the most difficult provisions of the law for people who were charged with the responsibility of protecting pharmaceutical patents was the fact that whatever the generic said it was going to do in the letter they sent the owner of the patent (referred to as a Notice Letter), regardless of whether it was true, had to be accepted. For example, if a generic company said it was going to use X process to make its generic product, the research-based company had to accept that as a true statement in making its decision whether or not it had a basis to sue the generic company for infringement of one of its patents.

If it turned out that the generic product was, in fact, made by an infringing process, then a lawsuit could be brought at that time. But the problem with this was by then it was too late. The generic product was already on the market, and it was difficult, if not impossible, to get an injunction. The toothpaste was already out of the tube.

* * *

Our Lipitor team included Peter, several attorneys, a paralegal and me. One of the attorneys was Will, who was not only the youngest but also, in key ways, the smartest. He had come to Pfizer from one of the most prestigious law firms in New York City. A Peter Pan of sorts, he saw no reason to get married and have children or to embrace any other of the accepted social conventions. His spirit roved freely, and his interests ranged from astrology to art. His youthful vitality delighted us all. And he was a very, very good patent litigator.

The second attorney on our team was Charlotte. Sharp as a whip and a ferocious litigator, she was also a classy dresser with good taste and a preference for Gucci shoes. A bit of a mother hen, she took care of us and made sure we all remembered each other's birthdays, as well as ensuring that our team room was stocked with the necessary supplies. Drop-dead gorgeous, she dazzled, and her charms had not gone unnoticed by Will. If I was ever in a hurry to find him, all I needed to do was find Charlotte. But he never allowed his infatuation with her—if that's what it was—to interfere with work. Most important, she was a very skilled patent litigator too.

Peter was more than twenty years older than most of us. He had been in the patent business for three decades and had the kind of wisdom that comes only with experience. Not only was he brilliant in an academic sense, he also possessed a powerful gut instinct not unlike my own when it came to litigation—an instinct that we had all learned to respect and honor over the years. He was our leader, our father, our mentor, and our protector. We could not have had or wished for a better boss.

There was one little thing about him that nagged at me, though. When I first started working with Peter, I noticed he wore a three-piece navy blue suit and crisp white shirt to work every single day. I finally asked him about it.

"Peter, have you ever thought of maybe changing things around a bit? Perhaps a sports jacket and slacks?"

He looked at me as if I had taken leave of my senses.

"That would take too much thinking about getting dressed in the morning. Anyway, I do change things around. Some of my suits are black or dark gray."

Peter was an American now, but he had been born and raised in England. Every now and then his British background would slip into his verbal communications. For example, whenever he said "at all," it came out as "a tall." And it took me a little while to learn that when he said something was "quite nice," he meant he didn't like it at all.

He was Mr. Predictable. Mr. Reliable. Over the course of the years, that reliability was a quality I had come to cherish. Now, as we embarked on the biggest litigation case the two of us would ever handle together, it was a quality I appreciated, and needed beyond all others, in a law partner.

Our paralegal was Carol Ann Williams. Carol had started off as my assistant and had risen through the professional ranks of the company, along the way obtaining her paralegal certificate and her college degree with an impressive 3.8 GPA. She was competent, smart, and hard-working, and I knew she would be a valuable addition to our group.

And there was me. I was the only attorney in our group of two hundred who was not also a scientist. In large measure by serendipity, I had fallen into patent litigation years before, but over time, thanks to Peter and members of my team, I had learned the chemistry. My fluency in French and Spanish proved to be useful in some of our international cases—one very high profile case in France, in particular. But the main asset I brought to our group, other than my work ethic, was my gut instinct. Somehow, I almost always knew what path to follow to win a case and which traps to avoid so as not to lose it.

New York City is home to some very skilled patent litigators, but in the end, we chose a lawyer from a Delaware firm—Connolly, Bove, Lodge and Hutz, to act as our outside counsel. Rudy Hutz was an impressive man. At six-foot-four, he cut an imposing figure, but, as far as I was concerned, his height did not match the power of his intellect or the depth of his spirit. He was practicing patent law when most of us were still in grade school; he was then, and still remains, one of the most skilled litigators in this field, having an uncanny ability to remain calm when the bullets are flying around the battlefield.

* * *

The forty-five days passed quickly. It's an indisputable fact about work and deadlines: No matter how much time you have to complete any given task, or how simple it may be, you will always be scrambling around, trying to finish it on the last day, up to the last minute. When Rudy confirmed that our complaint had been filed on February 21, I knew that the lawsuit against Ranbaxy, soon to spread to every major country on every major continent, had officially begun.

But what I didn't know—what I couldn't have suspected—was that a war within my own soul, and with it the emergence of a carefully guarded childhood secret, had begun as well. It would be this war within my heart that would take me to the brink of despair before it delivered me one day, battered and bruised but not completely defeated, to a place of joy. Despite the magnitude and financial importance of the outcome of the biggest patent infringement case of all time, the war inside my own being would prove to be far more life-changing for me than anything that transpired in the corporate world.

CHAPTER 4 - INTERNATIONAL CONFLICT
New York City, April 2003-February 2004

While we were busy dealing with the Ranbaxy challenge to Lipitor, Pfizer was attending to its second major merger in three years. In 2000 we had merged with Warner-Lambert. Now we were merging with Pharmacia.

Pfizer and Pharmacia began operating as a unified company on April 16, 2003. Pfizer's press announcement highlighted the fact that the combined company was now one of the world's fastest-growing and most valuable enterprises with a research budget of $7.1 billion. Hank McKinnell's statement added a little more information about Pfizer's hope for the future.

"Today we go forward as a single company providing more products to help more patients than any other pharmaceutical company has ever done before. On any given day, we estimate that nearly 40 million people around the world are treated with a Pfizer medicine. Our new company is the global leader in discovering, developing and delivering innovative medicines and health care solutions essential to improving global public health and addressing unmet medical needs."

* * *

The Lipitor case was complicated and involved complex chemistry. Like your hands, the Lipitor molecule exists in two mirror-image forms. These are called enantiomers. An equal amount of the two enantiomers is a racemic mixture. As a general rule, only one of the two enantiomers is therapeutically active and suitable for use as a pharmaceutical product.

Lipitor had three main patents listed in the FDA Orange Book, a compilation of pharmaceutical drugs and the patents covering them. The first—the basic patent—would expire in March 2010. The second—the enantiomer patent—would expire in July 2011. The third—the crystalline patent—would expire in 2017. When Pfizer filed suit against Ranbaxy, we sued on both the basic and enantiomer patents.

Generic companies didn't, as a general rule at this point in time, begin challenges by attacking basic product patents. But that, in effect, was what Ranbaxy was doing. Ranbaxy's letter advised us that they were seeking immediate marketing approval to sell a copycat Lipitor product, claiming that they did not infringe our patents and/or that they were invalid.

Ranbaxy had an important ally on its side—public opinion.

The pharmaceutical industry had supplanted the tobacco industry as Public Enemy Number One. It would be another five years before the big bad guy torch would pass to the banking industry. The glory days of the early '80s were long gone. If our stock had been rising like the mercury in a thermometer on a hot August day back then, it was sinking in the dead of winter now.

* * *

After we filed our complaint against Ranbaxy in the United States, we'd learned that they had also challenged our Lipitor patents in the U.K. Charlotte appeared in my office announcing the news. All I could do was shake my head and laugh. Charlotte didn't. Instead, she turned on the heels of her Gucci shoes and left, muttering something under her breath.

The rest of the European markets were soon under attack, as well, followed by Canada, Australia, New Zealand and the major Asian markets. Litigation in general is a bit like playing chess. International litigation is akin to playing a three dimensional form of it.

Ranbaxy had already launched copycat products in the lesser-developed countries, too. In essence, they were saying, "Catch us if you can," and snubbing their noses at our patents in those countries. With neither the courts nor the police on our side, we'd get no assistance from local authorities in those markets. Fact was, very few people were on our side anymore. Big Pharma was seen as Big Bad Pharma. Political ads of poor, little grandmothers having to choose between their medicine and food abounded.

I was determined to win the case. Peter was too. But he didn't mince his words, however, when my determination became too intense for an office environment.

"I've seen you win lawsuits by the sheer strength of your will and determination. But you are indeed the most headstrong and stubborn person I have ever known."

"Yes, it's true," I had to agree.

Although my Crouching Tiger, Hidden Dragon moniker was new, the behavior that had earned it lay deep in my personal history. My dad often recalled how, when I was two years old, I used to fall off the monkey bars, and each time I did, I'd get so furious that I would hold my breath until I passed out. Nothing my father would say or do could make me stop, until the day I had pulled my breath-holding stunt and fainting trick one too many times. My father had held me upside down by my ankles in a cold shower. When I'd come to, I was giggling and laughing. I think my love of the water and swimming was born that day, and my fall-and-faint routine ended. I never held my breath again . . . except in that relay race when I was bound and determined to win for my team.

While I'd not outgrown the challenge of metaphoric monkey bars, I was for sure too big to be held upside down by my ankles in a cold shower any longer. Nevertheless, I recognized that my intensity was not helping my group in particular or the workplace atmosphere in general. I was stubborn and willful, and I fought against institutional control because I found it almost as punishing and suffocating as what I had endured as a child.

I wasn't stupid. I knew I should have played the corporate game.

I certainly knew how.

I just could not force myself to do it.

CHAPTER 5 - YELLOW EYES
New York City, February–May 2004

Lipitor was only one of several high profile cases on which our group was working. Another such case involved our drug, Norvasc, and the Indian generic company, Dr. Reddy's. Norvasc was the number one treatment for hypertension and Pfizer's number two drug behind Lipitor.

Peter and I were flying back from a business meeting in Florida when the news of the decision arrived. It had been a year since we'd argued the case before the Court of Appeals in Washington, D.C, having lost it in the court below. The plane was descending through the clouds, and New York City lay glistening below in patches of winter sun. A quick glance around the crowded cabin assured me that no flight attendants were nearby. I switched on my BlackBerry ahead of landing.

A news alert jumped out at me like a Times Square neon sign. We had won the Dr. Reddy's case on appeal by a narrow two-to-one vote. All the waiting and uncertainty had ended while we'd been up in the air—literally.

The *New York Times* had already picked up the story.

"Pfizer, the drug maker, won a federal appeals court ruling that bars Dr. Reddy's Laboratories from selling a version of Pfizer's $4-billion-a-year hypertension drug Norvasc. The United States Court of Appeals for the Federal Circuit in Washington overturned a judge's ruling permitting Dr. Reddy's to sell a different chemical version than the Pfizer medicine. Norvasc, introduced in 1990, ranks No.4 in worldwide drug sales."

Putting on my best poker face, I pushed my BlackBerry toward Peter.

"You're not supposed to have that on."

I shook the BlackBerry and gestured with my eyes for him to take it from me.

"You're breaking the rules again, and I will not be your accomplice."

I gave him an oh brother shrug and pushed the device under his nose. He reluctantly read the message and smiled. I smiled too and wondered what big news would be next.

It wasn't at all what I'd expected, and this time it was literally a matter of life or death.

* * *

"Come on, Peter."

"What?"

"It's St. Paddy's Day. Let's give ourselves a lunch break. Drink some green ale."

I never had to ask Peter twice to go to lunch, especially if it promised to include a beer.

"You've twisted my arm. But you can drink the green beer. Guinness will do fine for me."

We hurried through the still-cold New York streets to a nearby Irish pub on Lexington Avenue. We escaped the dismal weather outside, and settled into the warm and welcoming, if very crowded, space. We found our way to a small table. Our waitress handed us menus, and we ordered our beers. I scanned the usual fare—corned beef and cabbage, shepherd's pie—before looking up from my menu to ask Peter a question. Tight as our space was, I was able to see his eyes quite clearly as they moved left to right across his menu. I looked away for a second, blinked, and then looked back at his eyes again. I followed his pupils, and as he read the menu I studied the whites of his eyes more closely. Except they weren't white. They were tinged a distinct shade of yellow.

I hesitated to point it out, yet . . .

Something was wrong, I felt it.

"Peter."

He looked up.

"I think I'll have sausage and mash. What about you?"

"Your eyes are yellow."

"What are you talking about?"

"Take off your glasses, please."

I leaned forward and peered into his eyes, which were even clearer now that he had removed his spectacles.

"Look over to your right for a second."

He did.

"Your eyes are yellow."

Leaning back in my chair, I blinked my own eyes in an effort to correct what I was seeing in his. Peter stood up.

"I'll go check them out in the bathroom mirror. Be right back."

He pushed his way through the crowded bar and toward the men's room door. I waited. The waitress appeared with our beers. I ordered food for both of us. I waited. I sipped my beer. And waited. Finally, I felt his presence and looked over my shoulder. I managed a halfhearted smile. He appeared calm, but he started speaking before he sat down.

"I don't think so, Traci. They don't look yellow to me."

I decided not to push it.

"Maybe it's the light in here."

No maybe about it; it wasn't the light: His eyes were yellow.

That Friday, Peter didn't come into the office. An email from him told me he'd had a conversation with his wife, Trudi, the night before.

"She thinks my eyes are yellow too. And she also thinks my skin is a bit yellowish."

I wrote back immediately, "Make a doctor's appointment."

Ignoring email protocol, I finished the sentence by typing in screaming capital letters:

"TODAY!"

Despite what I had seen, despite what his wife had seen, and despite what he himself had probably seen in the pub's bathroom mirror, Peter was still in denial.

"But you said it was the light in the restaurant!"

I typed a blunt reply.

"I lied."

* * *

The following week, his doctor scheduled a test to determine the cause of Peter's jaundice. They'd hoped it was gallbladder stones blocking the bile duct, but when Peter called after the endoscopic procedure the following week, I knew it was bad news before he'd got the first words out.

"It's not just stones."

"Well, what is it then?"

"It's not good, Traci."

"Peter, what do you have?"

"I have a really good chance . . ."

"Peter!"

"I need surgery."

I wanted to scream at him. I whispered instead.

"What is it?"

Silence. The quietest and longest silence ever.

"Pancreatic cancer."

"Oh, God."

I don't remember the rest of the conversation. We hung up. I frantically opened my laptop and fired it up. The little spinning wheel seemed to whirl forever. Come on, come on. As the icons blinked onto the screen, I hit Safari. Then I hit the Google search button.

Pancreatic cancer.

The first statistic I saw was the survival rate.

Less than four percent.

The next statistic was the average number of months from diagnosis to death.

Three.

I felt faint and leaned over my desk. I could feel the blood draining from my face, the bile rising in my throat. Then I proceeded to throw up.

All over my desk.

All over my chair.

All over myself.

As I stood in the stench of my distress, all I could think was "Why Peter?"

* * *

Because the disease is so deadly, there was not a moment to spare. The following Monday, April 2, was Peter's sixty-second birthday. It was also the day he walked over to the hospital with Trudi and checked himself in for the Whipple operation, a procedure that removes the cancerous parts of the pancreas. Peter would be in good hands. Memorial Sloan Kettering is one of the world's leading cancer centers. We had a brief email exchange before he left his apartment.

"Happy birthday!"

"Thanks, see you soon."

That was it. Hour after hour, I imagined Peter lying unconscious on a sterile operating table, fighting for his life. The surgery, scheduled for 10:00 a.m., had been postponed twice and had not started until after 5:00 p.m. It was close to midnight before I received word from Peter's son that the surgery was over and had gone well. Peter stayed in the hospital for the next week with Trudi by his side. He would often awake before daybreak to find her sleeping in the chair beside his bed.

But, as it happened, the operation was the "easy" part of Peter's ordeal. The doctors gave him a month to recuperate before his real battle began.

"There's likely to be some further unpleasantness," he had told me after the surgery, trying to minimize the reality of what lay ahead.

The unpleasantness combined an experimental cocktail of three different chemo agents with daily doses of radiation. For the next month I visited Peter almost every day, taking a briefcase full of work with me in an attempt to engage his mind in an external battle rather than the one that was raging within his body.

* * *

Six weeks after the surgery Peter tried to come back to the office. His first day was difficult; the second day, impossible. We were having what we'd later refer to as our Last Supper in the company cafeteria, and Peter was struggling to get down some soup. The chemo cocktail was devastating.

I couldn't bear witnessing his pain.

"Go home, Peter. You can't work right now."

He'd already lost thirty pounds; not overweight to begin with, he was now alarmingly thin. I expected him to fight me—with a dismissive wave of his hand in the air while insisting, "I'm fine." Instead, he put down his spoon, looked me in the eye, stood up, walked away, and left. He didn't say goodbye.

For nearly two months, Peter endured his ordeal in silence. Stoic to a fault, he never complained. Then one night, he collapsed. He was rushed to the emergency room at Sloan Kettering, where even the admitting doctor was shocked to see the list of chemo agents he'd been prescribed. Now back in the hospital for yet another extended stay, Trudi resumed her selfless vigil at his bedside.

For the second time in less than two months, Peter was fighting for his life. Although I realized the doctors had very little choice, as far as I was concerned, the amount of chemo they had pumped into his frail body had all but killed him.

This wonderful, caring man had been my best friend, my confidant, my teacher, my boss, and my advisor for the past twenty years. Here we were about to engage in the biggest legal battle of our careers, and for the first time in my professional life, I'd have to march into it without Peter.

I had two choices: to keep marching or ask to be taken off the case. For me, there was only one choice. There was only ever one choice.

It would have been reasonable to say that I was unable to focus on the Lipitor case due to Peter's illness—that his absence placed on me the burden of our whole group's management. With Peter on an extended, if not permanent, leave of absence, I could have bowed out. Or I could have taken my turn at bat.

In my head, I heard my father's words, mirroring those of Nelson Mandela, about courage and fear.

"Traci, courage is not the absence of fear; it's marching directly into the face of it."

So I marched.

I picked up my bat with steadfast determination and walked up to home plate.

And the only time I ever looked back was to check on Peter.

CHAPTER 6 – SMALL SACRIFICES
New York City, June-July 2004

All mergers bring turmoil.

Ours were no exception.

With the merger between Pfizer and Pharmacia now complete, we had to shift our focus for a while from the escalating drama surrounding the Lipitor case to a whole new set of issues.

New people, new products, new problems.

The merger brought a lot of new patent cases for our group to manage. Pharmacia's Celebrex product alone had dozens of patent infringement cases pending around the world, not to mention a well-publicized battle with the University of Rochester in the U.S. But the Pharmacia merger also introduced us to one of the best teams of IP litigators around, Jack Blumenfeld and Maryellen Noreika, from the Morris Nichols firm in Wilmington, who were handling Pharmacia's patent case over Xalatan.

* * *

Things had changed a lot since the good old days— indeed, our days of wine and roses, or, perhaps more accurately, of wine and picnics. Our motto had been "The Pfizer Family," and it had felt very much like we were all part of one big, happy, extended family unit. We'd all felt safe. The scientists in research discovered one blockbuster after another. Their creative energy, as well as their genius, flowed freely and flooded our pipeline with promising new pharmaceutical candidates that were destined to help millions of patients.

We actually had an annual Pfizer family picnic at the local amusement park. We also received holiday presents from the company each December—gifts that we were invited to preselect from a brightly-colored catalog that appeared in our in-boxes each fall.

The '80s were the golden years of the pharmaceutical industry in general. We were the darlings of Wall Street. Our stock split and split again. Our position in the economy, it seemed, was invincible. The U.S. government supported Big Pharma. In the global arena, the pharmaceutical industry succeeded in getting the world's first international treaty on IP standards, Trade Related Intellectual Property (TRIPs), enacted, which, for the first time, afforded strong intellectual property rights to innovators around the world.

Pfizer's CEO was Ed Pratt, a man with more charisma and charm than anyone I'd ever met. Best of all, he took good care of all the Pfizer employees. I was no exception. After spending my first four years at Pfizer in human resources (HR), where I'd helped set up the company's Employee Assistance Program, I was seeking to break into the legal division. Though I'd been happy in HR, I was now ready to start officially practicing law. I'd applied for an entry level job in the legal department; I was rejected and decided to quit. It was Pratt who had intervened on my behalf and convinced the general counsel to find a spot for me.

I'd started off at the bottom, but a series of lucky breaks took me in short order up to the position of general counsel for the company's European affairs. I'd found myself facing my first patent case—and Peter. I was twenty-nine years old and pregnant. Peter was forty-three—as good as ancient from my twenty-something point of view, but I was soon to discover that he had enough energy to run circles around me.

After my son, Chad, was born, Peter and I had started traveling all over Europe. Tackling one problem after another, we'd often hit three different countries in a single day. Breakfast meetings in Brussels were followed by late afternoon lunch meetings in Paris, which were topped off by dinner meetings in Madrid. It was heady and exciting, except that my conscience was nagging me. I was now a mother, and Jackie O's famous words were echoing in my ears.

"If you mess up being a good parent, nothing else you ever do in life really matters."

I felt I could not continue to be a big-time lawyer and even a halfway decent mother, so I chose to give up my job as European general counsel and work part-time. It was not an easy decision. I had been featured in a recent *Fortune* magazine's "People to Watch" column. I knew I was on the fast track to the top. I had battled my way into law school, battled my way into the legal division, battled my way through pregnancy, and now I was turning my back on all my hard won victories and walking away. But I was going to give my child what my mother had denied me: attention and time.

* * *

The glory days of the '80s ceded to the economic turbulence of the '90s. William Jefferson Clinton was elected president in November 1992. Soon after taking office he created a task force on national healthcare reform. Drug prices were an easy target, and the government had focused its attention on the pharmaceutical industry. The effect was subtle at first, but our industry's fall from grace had begun. Painful though it was for us on many levels, it was also already apparent—some twenty years before Obamacare had become a national debate and a household word—that the issue of healthcare costs needed to be addressed in the U.S.

A decade later, Big Pharma's troubles were multiplying. Pipelines were running dry. Mergers and cost-cutting measures had become the norm. In our now resource-constrained environment, top-level executives were jockeying for power. After a merger, there were often two chiefs for every top job but only one teepee. Political duels are never quick or easy, and in the messy process of selecting a clear winner, the supporting troops were sometimes lost along the way.

Protect your king.

Even if it means sacrificing your queen.

CHAPTER 7 - SIMPLIFY
New York City, August-November 2004

With Peter on sick leave, the workload of our group increased. We spent every single day, weekends included, preparing for the U.S. Lipitor trial. Our labors were made more difficult by the never-ending media speculation about the upcoming trial. These concerns were affecting our stock price, as well as our nerves, as the headline on the August 21 *New York Times* article made clear.

"Pfizer Falls on Concern over Generic Drug Threat."

Smith Barney's drug analyst, George Grofik, was quoted as saying that Ranbaxy's challenge to the Lipitor patents should not be dismissed as "frivolous."

"After reviewing the relevant court documents and consulting our patent attorney, we believe there are significant risks to the Lipitor patent estate," he said in a report.

Grofik did, however, temper his viewpoint with the realism about the complexity and difficulty of any patent litigation.

"Patent law is subtle and complex, making the outcome of Ranbaxy's Lipitor challenge far from certain."

* * *

We felt fortunate that Joseph J. Farnan, a smart and fair judge, had been assigned to the case; he was one of very few

U.S. judges with extensive experience in the esoteric area of patent infringement litigation.

Judge Farnan, however, enforced one particular rule that would dictate how we presented our case. He allowed our trial to run for only two weeks, period. Each side was granted one week—and not a single hour more—in which to present its case.

Judge Farnan kept a timer in the courtroom, reminding us that every single minute we were on our feet, whether on direct examination or cross, we were depleting the precious time we'd been allotted. It could be pretty unnerving.

I didn't mind Judge Farnan's rule, however, as I believed that the quantity of work paralleled the amount of time allotted to do it. If the judge had allowed us one month to present our case, we'd have taken a month, as would have Ranbaxy. The brevity imposed upon us could work to our advantage. But the challenge before us was enormous.

Simplify, simplify, simplify, said Thoreau.

Patent infringement litigation is where science and art collide. Any trained litigator knows that it is difficult to win a case if the story is too complicated. Complexity fosters frustration, then disinterest, followed by boredom, and finally anger. You lose the judge, you lose the case. So we had to keep it simple. But simplicity was not always easy to achieve when dealing with stereoselective chemistry.

For example, it took me a while to fully grasp what an enantiomer molecule was because both the left and right-handed ones look identical when drawn on a piece of paper. I was finally able to understand one day, however, as I hurried from my office and picked up my left glove and accidentally tried to put it on my right hand. You can't put a left-handed glove on your right hand any more than you can shake the right hand of a person using your left hand. The right mirrors the left.

* * *

In the middle of September the Public Patent Foundation (PUBPAT), a not-for-profit organization whose stated mission is to protect freedom in the patent system, jumped into the action when it filed a formal request with the Patent Office to revoke our Lipitor crystalline patent. Peter, despite his frail physical nature, had a fit when he heard about it, which I took as a good sign that he'd be back to work soon.

Peter did return to work a short time thereafter. Still on chemo medications, he wore a pump to render continuous doses of fluorouracil, an anticancer drug known as 5-FU. He could almost hide the pump under his navy blue blazer, which had long since replaced the jacket of his three-piece navy blue suit. I continued to read pancreatic cancer survival statistics as if I were studying for a calculus exam. While in my heart I believed that Peter would indeed be among the fortunate four percent who survived, my mind was shadowed with doubt.

And fear.

* * *

The middle of November brought us the first piece of encouraging news, however. Peter had been relieved of his chemo pump. It had been eight months since his diagnosis, and his scans thus far had been clean.

"I'm going to make it!" he exclaimed when he called to tell me.

I wasn't sure whether he was referring to the upcoming Lipitor trial or to his own survival, but at that moment it didn't matter.

He was alive.

"Are you up for celebrating the removal of your 5-FU pump? What about dinner tonight?"

The weather was beautiful and warm despite the lateness of the season.

"We can even eat outside if you want."

If there was any hesitation on his part, it was fleeting.

"Yes. Let's do that, Traci."

We had promised ourselves an evening free from any discussion of Lipitor, but we found it difficult to talk about anything else. Having the benefit of Peter's presence, and of his counsel, however brief, was almost overwhelming. As much as I didn't want the night to end, I could see that Peter was growing tired. We paid the bill and left. Out on the sidewalk people were strolling with their coats over their arms, enjoying a late Indian summer night.

"Should we share a cab?" I asked.

"No. Let's walk," he suggested.

We'd not quite reached Peter's place when he stopped. He looked at me in despair.

"Traci, I can't take one more step."

A known unpleasant side effect of 5-FU is sore feet—on occasion, really sore feet, due to the blisters caused by the drug. Putting Peter's left arm over my shoulder, I turned myself into a human crutch.

"Lean on me."

He managed a smile.

"I already do."

A lump rose in my throat, and my legs wobbled. I cleared my throat; I willed my feet to keep walking and my words to be steadfast and encouraging.

"We'll get you home," I promised, and together we hobbled toward his apartment.

Once I'd seen Peter into the lobby of his building, I walked back out to Lexington Avenue. Yellow taxis and city buses were speeding by, and I sat down on the curb—and wept—out of frustration, out of fear, out of self-pity, out of self-loathing. Witnessing again the devastation of Peter's cancer and chemo treatment, which had taken him to death's door, was a stark reminder that none of us, no matter how fast we run, can escape life's great leveler. For the first time in years, I was also reminded of something else—a secret I'd hidden from my closest friends. Even Peter did not yet know the truth. But sitting on the curb that November night, I knew with one hundred percent certainty that sooner or later, just as Peter was doing now, I would have to face my demons, as well.

CHAPTER 8 - TRIAL
Wilmington, Delaware, November–December 2004

The team set off for Wilmington after the Thanksgiving holiday. The train ride afforded us a brief respite from our labors; so, I slept. Upon our arrival, we met in our team room in Rudy's office. The following morning, we gathered for an early breakfast. When we finished our second, or third, cup of coffee, I surveyed our team—Peter, Will, Charlotte, Rudy and his partners—with a hopeful smile.

"Okay, let's rock and roll."

The morning was crisp. The sky was clear; the late fall sun shone. We decided to walk to the courthouse, but we barely spoke. A determined silence swaddled us.

The U.S. marshals at the security gates checked our IDs, and we entered Wilmington's small federal courthouse. With only three sitting judges at the time, we located the room where our case would be heard with ease. Inside, the first person I saw was Ranbaxy's general counsel, Jay Deshmukh. Tall and lean, indeed a towering presence, he was hard to miss. I wondered if he'd played basketball in high school or college.

Well, game on.

The Pfizer contingent and supporters settled into the right side of the courtroom; Ranbaxy's detachment positioned itself on the left. It reminded me of the seating at a wedding, except we were not there to celebrate bonds and bliss.

Judge Farnan entered, and we stood to show our respect as he approached the bench. Like most courtrooms, Judge Farnan's was somber and formal, with dark wood paneling—the "bar" in its center separating the spectators from the lawyers, witnesses, and court officials. One is "admitted to the bar" not only in a figurative sense but also quite literally, as only lawyers who have been certified to practice law in a particular court are allowed to step beyond the bar—in this instance, for our side, Rudy and his partners, who were licensed in the state of Delaware.

During the trial of another of our cases, Will, in his excitement, had once lunged over the bar to tell Pfizer's lawyer, Joe O'Malley, that we would post the bond required to secure the preliminary injunction the judge had just granted us. The judge had been so startled by the sudden appearance of Will on the wrong side of the bar that he'd not had time to issue an admonishment before Will had flung himself back into his spectator's seat.

In his long, dark robe, Judge Farnan was an imposing figure at his bench. He assumed the formality of the courtroom he ruled; you could tell that he was a no-nonsense judge. When the Lipitor case hit his docket, he had already served as a federal judge for almost twenty years, having been nominated by President Reagan in 1985. (When he would retire in 2010, he would be the longest-serving judge on the federal bench in Delaware.)

The clerk reminded us of the rules of court—no eating, no photographs, and all the usual mandates, with emphasis on Judge Farnan's signature pet peeve.

No cell phones.

Anyone who violated this rule would be asked to leave the courtroom and not return. Though cell phones annoyed Judge Farnan, that other ubiquitous product of technology did not. Throughout the trial, he appeared to be looking at the computer screen on his bench. You might have thought he was not paying attention until the moment he would raise his head and ask a pertinent, searing question. It was soon clear to all of us that he was brilliant.

Rudy had barely started his opening statement when it happened.

A cell phone rang, as clear and crisp as a bell. His ears pricked, Judge Farnan lifted his gaze from his computer screen. He was not pleased.

"Excuse me for a minute. A little while ago, someone's electronic device went off on this side of the courtroom."

Silence.

"Whoever that was, could you stand up please?"

More silence.

"Am I the only one that heard that device go off?? Anybody over here hear it? Whoever's device it is ought to stand up now and go with the Court security officer, or else everybody is going to leave the courtroom."

No one moved.

Then low level scuffling. Heads began turning in one direction, to single out the violator in their midst. The young, blond man looked more like a college student than the reporter he was. Slowly, reluctantly, he raised his hand.

"Your Honor, I think it might have been my hearing aid," he stammered in a weak attempt to excuse his transgression.

Judge Farnan bore no excuses.

"All right. You go with the Court security officer and let them check that out. Thank you."

Rudy was clearly amused.

"Your ears are very good, Your Honor. I frankly didn't hear it."

"I apologize for interrupting you," Judge Farnan replied with a slight twinkle in his eye.

"Not at all. Not at all," Rudy assured him that there was no problem on his end.

And the young, blond man was marched to the end of the plank—well, escorted out of the courtroom anyway—and that, as Judge Farnan had promised, was the last we'd see of him.

* * *

The presentation of a patent infringement case is long and complicated, and we had only one week to do it. And there were two patents in this case—the basic, expiring in 2010, and the enantiomer, expiring in 2011—each one of which could have been the subject of a trial in and of itself.

Rudy presented our witnesses, including Bruce Roth, the inventor of Lipitor, and his pharmacology colleague, Roger Newton. I was enamored with the idea that one of our scientists was named Newton, and jokingly referred to him as Sir Isaac. Each time one of our witnesses was sworn in and promised to tell "the truth, the whole truth and nothing but the truth," I silently joined in with the refrain, "So help me, God."

Ranbaxy's counsel cross-examined each of our witnesses after Rudy was done. They spent most of their time with Roth on the basic patent. Even though it is the job of any good counsel to try and discredit the other side's witness, there was still an air of respect in the courtroom for the man who had discovered the greatest pharmaceutical product of all time.

Next up was Roger Newton. After establishing that Newton was the head of the atherosclerosis (coronary heart disease) drug discovery team at Warner Lambert, Ranbaxy's counsel asked him to turn his attention to the scientific studies we had presented into evidence.

Q: Is that your signature?

A: Yes.

Q: What responsibility did you have for these documents?

A: I had primary responsibility to distribute this as the chairman of the atherosclerosis drug discovery team and also to review the pharmacology section.

Q: What kind of information was presented in the pharmacology section of these reports?

A: That is AICS data, the acute inhibition of cholesterol synthesis screen.

Q: Do you know why that was included in this report?

A: The reason it was included was because the racemic lactone, which was a lead compound, had poor bioavailability.

Q: Now was management interested in this two-fold difference?

A: Not at all, not at all. Their interest was whether the single enantiomer was actually bioavailable and doing its job.

Q: Did you understand at the time that that data to be a quantitative comparison of the inherent inhibitory activity for those compounds?

A: No, not at all. It doesn't show that whatsoever. The purpose of this is to show which of these compounds is more bioavailable.

Q: At the time you signed off on this report, would you have considered the results of these experiments to be in any way inconsistent with a ten-fold difference shown in the CSI assay?

A: They are two different experiments. Their objectives are totally different. This is observational data. This could be two, it could be ten, it could be fifteen, it could be a hundred. The most important thing that we show here is that the chiral calcium salt was more potent and bioavailable.

Q: Turn back to the results section if you will. The second sentence under the results section states: This is to be expected if 50 percent of the racemic salt is the inactive isomer. Do you see that?

A: Uh-huh, I do.

Q: Did you agree with that statement at the time you signed this document?

A: Well there is a qualifier here.

Q: Dr. Newton did you testify during your deposition that Warner Lambert later proved the assumption that ... all of the biological activity resided in the ... enantiomer.

A: Biological activity has many meanings, many meanings.

Q: And during...

A: Let me finish please. If you're talking about inherent inhibitory activity as far as affecting cholesterol synthesis, it was inactive.

Q: Did Pfizer also determine, based on its in vitro screens, that essentially all of the activity was contained in the enantiomer?

A: That's a—your answer has virtually all. What does that mean? I don't know what that means. That's not a scientific term, that's a qualified term, and I'm not going to answer that question unless you define what you mean.

We took a break.

* * *

The next two weeks saw a continuous parade of other witnesses—experts in chemistry, medicine, drug sales, among others—and despite the intense and long days, the days allotted for trial passed quickly. Before we knew it the time arrived for closing arguments arrived. Rudy summarized our most salient points, and we packed up and headed out. It was a long walk back to the hotel to get our bags—a long walk made longer by the uncertainty of when Judge Farnan would issue his decision, as well as the news that hit my Blackberry the day before—the U.S. Patent Office had granted PUPBAT's request and ordered a reexamination of the Lipitor crystalline patent.

The trial in Wilmington had exhausted us. Nevertheless, we now had to prepare our response in the reexamination of our crystalline patent. *Law360* was quick to pick up the news on December 8.

"In a troubling development for Pfizer Inc., the U.S. Patent and Trademark Office has agreed to reexamine the drug maker's patent on the cholesterol-lowering treatment Lipitor, the world's best-selling drug. The USPTO issued its order based on a request by a small activist group, the Public Patent Foundation (PUBPAT), stating that the request raised 'a substantial new question of patentability' regarding all 44 claims of the patent.

Third-party requests for reexamination are successful in having the subject patent either narrowed or completely revoked roughly 70% of the time, according to USPTO statistics.

'This is the first step towards ending the significant financial and public health harms being caused to the public by this patent that should have never issued,' said Dan Ravicher, PUBPAT's Executive Director and Founder.

Ravicher said Pfizer has been exploiting the patent to litigate against generic drug companies to prevent consumers from legitimately obtaining atorvastatin, the generic name of the drug, whose one-month supply costs from $105 to $132 in New York."

The front page news of our trial in Wilmington and the upcoming reexamination of our crystalline patent left little doubt as to what was at stake. But what we didn't know, what we could not have suspected as 2004 mercifully drew to an end, was that we would all soon be tested in ways none of us could have imagined.

CHAPTER 9 - A LONG JOURNEY
New York City, January–May 2005

Will and Charlotte appeared in my door.

Will handed me a copy of the latest issue of *Corporate Counsel* magazine. Staring up at me from the cover of the December 30, 2004 issue was Ranbaxy's general counsel, Jay Deshmukh. The caption under his smiling face read, "Giant Slayer."

Big, bold letters.

I picked up the magazine and read the highlights.

"In a case that could shake the foundation of the pharmaceutical and biotech industries, New Delhi-based generic drug maker Ranbaxy Laboratories Limited claims that the main patent for Lipitor—Pfizer's biggest-selling product and the world's most lucrative drug—does not cover the form of a key ingredient used in the cholesterol-fighting drug. The suit also shines a spotlight on Deshmukh, an obscure, unassuming patent attorney who finds himself playing David to Pfizer's Goliath. He's a giant slayer with nerve to spare. Deshmukh has prodded his staid company—which was once content just to wait for patents on name-brand drugs to expire before it tried to sell generics—to brashly take on top-selling drugs like Lipitor. 'We don't do willy-nilly patent challenges,' Deshmukh says."

I rubbed my eyes and continued reading.

"Smith Barney analyst George Grofik told his clients, 'After reviewing the relevant court documents, we believe there are significant risks to the Lipitor patent estate.' Grofik changed his rating on Pfizer from . . . buy to hold."

I shrugged and handed the magazine back to Will who was standing next to Charlotte watching me read. Will mimicked my shrug and handed me a copy of a January 11 *Wall Street Journal* article. The headline told me that I would be reading more of the same.

"Challenge to Pfizer's Lipitor Has Some Investors Worried."

There was nothing I could do to alter the tide of analyst opinion. Virtually no one was predicting a win for Pfizer on both patents.

But the good news was unrelated to, and more important than, any business issue. The winter was warming into spring, and Peter was getting stronger by the month. He was putting on weight, his stamina was increasing, and his appetite was growing again, not only for food but for life and work as well. We hoped and prayed that the cancer would not return. Every time he went for a scan, we held our collective breath until we got the thumbs-up signal in his two word emails.

"All okay."

* * *

With the U.K. trial set to begin in July, our daily preparations were intensifying. I was deep in thought one afternoon when Carol Williams, our paralegal, came barging into my office out of breath.

"Here it is!"

She was waving the latest International Federation of Pharmaceutical Manufacturers Association publication in the air.

"Wow! So exciting!" I said, glancing at the colorful booklet that contained most of the data exclusivity laws around the world that Carol and I had compiled together over the years.

Data exclusivity laws establish the rules that generics must follow to obtain marketing approval. The project demonstrated again how indispensable Carol had become to the IPE team. She'd traveled far since she'd arrived at Pfizer.

Carol was born to humble means in Guyana in September 1959. At the age of eleven, she came to the United States. Her family's escape to the promise of a better life in America bore all the hallmarks of a classic immigrant's tale. A perhaps equally life-changing segment of her journey began in 1991, when she arrived in our legal division.

Pfizer had a roster of temp agencies that it used on a regular basis, and Carol worked for one of them. She had been temping from one job to another all over the city by the time she arrived at Pfizer, where she'd be working with me until my assistant recovered from surgery. When my assistant decided not to return, I offered Carol the job.

Although she'd be making less money at first as an employee than as a temp, she accepted my offer on the spot. We were both beaming when I handed her the official offer letter.

"Welcome aboard!"

Once she'd become a bona fide member of our team, it didn't take any of us long to realize that Carol was very special. Her story of triumph was made even more inspiring when one considers the difficulties she faced. She was not yet college-educated, but she did have one very important thing going for her. She was intelligent and motivated enough to work by day as my loyal assistant and by night to attend Marymount College. She was juggling the demands of a full-time job, college course work, two young children, and a husband. I often thought of the Booker T. Washington quote when I thought of Carol.

"Success is to be measured not so much by the position one has reached in life as by the obstacles which he has overcome."

At this point, under Will's direction, Carol had started functioning as an administrative contact for the Caribbean islands. Her persistence and passion for helping local management protect patents was making her something of a legend there. Once, upon disembarking from her plane in Jamaica, she had been greeted by a marching band in appreciation of a recent court victory.

Despite the continual cost-cutting measures and layoffs, Pfizer still tried to take care of the remaining employees, and a people-development initiative was begun. Carol was one of many employees who benefited from it. Kindler used to refer to Carol as "the poster child for the People Development Program." So inspiring to other women was her story that Pfizer produced a movie to document it: *The Carol Ann Williams Story: From Temp to Paralegal*, as well as a sequel a few years later. Carol delivered inspirational speeches about her life for the benefit of other Pfizer colleagues; hundreds of women would come to hear her story of persistence and success, despite the odds.

"Carol, have you ever considered going to law school?" I asked her one day after one of her speeches.

The way she looked at me, I knew she thought my idea was crazy. She didn't say no, however. She had fourteen years of work experience in the legal division at Pfizer, and Kindler's promise to write a personal letter of recommendation for her. She also had a 3.8 GPA from Marymount. She studied hard for her LSATs. With decent scores, she applied to half a dozen law schools in the area. I expected her to get in to any one of them.

She didn't.

Instead, she was waitlisted by all of them. A few months later, she received all the final rejection letters in the same week. Her LSAT scores were not quite strong enough for her to gain admission. She appeared in my office doorway and leaned against the doorjamb. I looked at her, she looked at me. Tears welled up, and we both started crying. Waves of guilt swept over me. Had I cast her into uncharted waters with no life preserver? I didn't know.

I did know that she wasn't done. I got up from my desk and shut the door. My favorite Winston Churchill "never give in" poster stared at us from the back of the door.

"Take the damn test again, Carol," I implored her.

She smiled; it was a sad smile. She shook her head.

"I can't, Traci. I'm really sorry, but I just can't. I'm too tired, too old, and too upset."

"Yes, you can!"

She had come so far. It was heartbreaking.

Her tears swelled again. I handed her a bunch of tissues. She dried her eyes, her head bent into her chest. When she looked up, though, she was smiling the Carol smile I had come to love. Brave. Hopeful. Full of faith. Determined.

"Okay, I'll take the test again!"

And with those few words, our tears of sadness were replaced with ones of joy. A journey that had begun as a dream in a faraway land so many years ago would continue with the same fundamental and all-important provisions for success—hope, courage, and a steadfast determination despite all odds.

CHAPTER 10 - WHITE WIGS AND BOMBS
London, June–July 2005

In June we received the news that the U.S. Patent Office had initially rejected our Lipitor crystalline patent in the patent reexamination proceedings. *PharmaTimes* carried a brief report on June 23.

"The U.S. Patent and Trademark Office has ruled that one of five key patents covering Pfizer's multi-billion dollar cholesterol-lowering agent, Lipitor (atorvastatin), are invalid.

The ruling came on the back of a challenge filed last year by the not-for-profit organization, The Public Patent Foundation, which says it 'represents the public's interests against the harms caused by the patent system, particularly the harms cause by wrongly issued patents and unsound patent policy.' The patent office rejected all 44 of the patent's claims. 'Revoking Pfizer's patent is a critical step towards providing American consumers with access to Lipitor at a fair price, which will not only provide substantial economic benefit, but will also improve public health, as even Pfizer admits that many Americans in need of the drug are not getting it,' said Dan Ravicher, PUBPAT's executive director."

* * *

We had little time to address it, however. We were soon on the red-eye out of JFK; we landed at London's Heathrow Airport the following morning. By noon, we'd set up our war room at our hotel just off the Strand. It was only a five-minute walk from the Royal Courts of Justice, or the Law Courts, as they're commonly known. After a quick shower and a bite to eat, a likewise quick walk took us to the office of our solicitor, Trevor Cook of Bird & Bird on Fetter Lane.

The U.K. legal system is different from that of the U.S. in many ways, most notably in that clients work with solicitors, who, in turn, work with barristers—the counsels who, white wigs and all, stand up in court to present the case. Our barrister was Mr. Simon Thorley, a well-respected Queen's Counsel.

After a full day of prepping for trial, we all went to a restaurant near Covent Garden for dinner and a much-needed round of drinks. The conviviality at least temporarily allayed my anxiety about the case, though the worry never really went away. Last-minute doubts and fears lurked in the shadows, like the waiters in the background eager for us to leave so they could close up and go home.

* * *

We rose early for the first day of the trial. Contrary to our expectations, the weather was quite pleasant—warm with no hint of rain—until it became downright hot. The court was not air-conditioned, and by late afternoon, the heat had become overwhelming.

Our case had been assigned to Mr. Justice Nicolas Pumfrey, a well-known and well-respected senior judge. His track record with patent cases, however, was not favorable to patentees.

Entering the ancient Law Courts in London is like time travel. Traditions that have been preserved for centuries, and for reasons best-known only by them, barristers and judges in curly white wigs don flowing black gowns and long robes. On this occasion, however, July had wrought a day so hot that even Justice Pumfrey allowed counsel to strip down to their

Savile Row suits—better that than having to cart a collapsed barrister or two out of the sweltering court.

Ranbaxy's contingent of defense lawyers was settling into position at their bench. Simon, Trevor, and Charlotte settled into ours. I spotted Deshmukh. He waved to me across the crowded gallery as he approached his team. I liked Deshmukh even though he worked for Ranbaxy. He was fair, honest, and a real gentleman—despite the fact that the company he represented was Ranbaxy.

"Hey, it's only business," Peter would say when my anger flared.

Only it wasn't.

As far as I was concerned, Lipitor belonged to Pfizer, Ranbaxy wanted to sell it, and we had to stop them.

* * *

On Thursday, July 21, we had a free morning. It provided an ideal opportunity for Peter and me to slip down to Pfizer's research site in the town of Sandwich and visit our colleagues for a few hours. Sandwich, a historic town close to Dover in the county of Kent, is where the 4th Earl of Sandwich concocted the snack that bears his name. By placing slices of cold beef between pieces of bread, he was able to sustain himself, it's said, without interruption at the gaming table for twenty-four hours. Clever man.

Although Pfizer did not announce the closing of the Sandwich R & D facility until February 2011, other Big Pharma companies had been announcing similar plant closures. It does not take a rocket scientist, or even a Pfizer scientist, to figure out that no research means no inventions, which means no need for attorneys to write patents. Sandwich may have its charms all the way down on the Kentish coast—a great place for seagulls and perhaps for sandwiches, but not so great for laid-off patent attorneys.

We set off early Thursday morning; our plan was to return to London in time for the afternoon session in court. Once there, we assured our colleagues that if and when the Sandwich site did close one day, we would do our best to find positions for them in other locations. Any consolation, though, was hollow. They had homes, spouses with jobs, kids in school—all in Sandwich. Relocation would disrupt and alter their well-ordered lives. Not even the prospect of working at the Pfizer site in Paris was reassuring or enticing.

* * *

We were concluding our morning session when the site manager's assistant walked in and passed him a note. I knew something was up, and that the something was not good, when, after reading it, he jerked his head up and looked in our direction.

"There's just been another terrorist bombing on the London Underground," he announced to the group. "Peter and Traci, I'm afraid all the roads in and out of London have been closed, and the police are not allowing any traffic in either direction."

"Shit," Peter said. "We need to get back to court by two p.m."

"We're not going to make it," I said matter-of-factly.

Security in London had already been tight. Only a few weeks earlier, four suicide terrorists had detonated bombs on several trains and a bus, killing fifty-two people. So Londoners' nerves were on edge even before that Thursday morning's bomb attempts.

Peter and I managed to hire a driver to take us back up the highway as far as the authorities allowed. In Orpington, a suburb in Surrey, we hopped on a local train to Charing Cross Station. Almost everyone else was heading in the opposite direction, of course, in a desperate attempt to flee London and escape the potential danger. We were traveling headlong into the chaos that they fled.

London had assumed the aura of a ghost town by the time we returned. It had been a long, bad day. There was nothing we could do about our missed afternoon court session and not much for our colleagues in Sandwich either. As we walked back to our hotel, I was overwhelmed by frustration.

Peter must have been sharing my disconsolation because we walked aimlessly, street by empty street, without exchanging so much as a single word. I had spent a lifetime shutting down my emotions to cope with what was happening in my environment, but even I was shocked by the level of "emergency room syndrome" we had developed. I wondered what else would need to go wrong that day before one or both of us would have lost it.

But we didn't. Instead we walked on, staring straight ahead, with no destination in mind.

The trial ended the next day. Exhausted, we headed back to New York to wait for the decision. When we landed at JFK airport, I turned on my BlackBerry. The hundreds of emails that had accumulated during our seven-hour flight across the Atlantic started loading. Many of them were asking me a version of the same question.

"Are we going to win?"

PART TWO: WINS AND LOSSES

Never give in. Never give in.
Never, never, never, never—in nothing,
great or small, large or petty—never
give in, except to convictions of honor
and good sense. Never yield to force.
Never yield to the apparently
overwhelming might of the enemy.
—Sir Winston Churchill

CHAPTER 11 – THE BRITISH INVASION
New York City, October-November, 2005

The summer of 2005 was hot, and things were heating up on all fronts. At the same time that we were waiting for the U.K. and U.S. decisions, additional Lipitor trials were being scheduled around the world.

Adding fuel to the flame beneath our boiling pot was the news that the U.K. decision would be issued on October 12. Justice Pumfrey was wasting no time. Times like these required nerves of steel.

This was our first Lipitor decision.

The world was watching.

The weeks sped by. Summer ceded to fall. October 12, Columbus Day, arrived with its celebrations of the Spanish discovery of the Americas. We hoped to be able to celebrate a discovery of our own: Justice Pumfrey's imminent decision regarding our case. The U.K. ruling was due to be announced at 3:00 p.m. in London. That was 10:00 a.m. in New York, but the inevitable calls and emails had begun coming in hours earlier. I had just emerged into Grand Central Terminal from my morning commute when my cell phone started beeping from the missed calls.

Even though I was only a few minutes from my office, I nevertheless stopped in the splendor of the station terminal by the ornate information booth to return a few of them. When I was finished, I picked up the bag that I had straddled while talking on my cell and stepped out onto 42nd Street. It was a beautiful day. I hoped it was going to stay that way once we'd received Charlotte's email from London.

I was in a conference room with floor-to-ceiling windows that allowed dazzling views of the East River when Charlotte's email finally arrived later that morning. It carried mixed news. We had won on the basic patent but lost on the enantiomer. The next day, the *New York Times* was among the many newspapers that carried the story.

"A British court provided a mixed verdict for Pfizer in a crucial patent dispute yesterday, upholding one of the company's British patents on Lipitor, the company's best-selling cholesterol-lowering medicine, but invalidating a second one.

The ruling, by Justice Nicholas Pumfrey of the High Court in London, will have no practical effect on Pfizer's control over Lipitor in Britain because the court upheld a patent that covers the main active ingredient in the drug.

That patent does not expire until November 2011. The patent the court invalidated had a shorter duration, expiring in July 2010, so Pfizer's exclusive right to sell Lipitor in Britain will stay intact until November 2011.

Shares of Pfizer, the world's biggest drug company, closed up more than 2 percent yesterday in the United States after the verdict was announced. Still, at $24.84, they are trading near an eight-year low, in part because of investors' concerns about a related Lipitor patent challenge in the United States, a far larger market.

If the American case were to be decided in the same way as the British one, Pfizer could lose its patent protection for Lipitor in this country about a year sooner than currently expected. Sales in the United States represent about 60 percent of the $12 billion global market for Lipitor, which is the world's best-selling drug and by some estimates accounts for nearly half of Pfizer's profits.

In a statement, Pfizer said it was generally pleased with the ruling but would appeal the part of the decision invalidating its 2010 patent, 'This is an important victory not only for Pfizer but for all innovators pursuing high-risk medical discoveries,' said Henry A. McKinnell, the company's chairman.

A decision in the United States patent case, which was tried last year before a federal judge in Delaware, is expected before the end of December, Pfizer and Ranbaxy say. As it did in Britain, Ranbaxy is arguing in the case in Delaware that Pfizer's basic patents on Lipitor, whose active ingredient is a chemical called atorvastatin, are invalid.

In this case, as in most patent lawsuits, the arguments are often complicated and highly technical. In essence, Ranbaxy has claimed that one of the two Lipitor patents does not cover the exact molecular form of atorvastatin that Pfizer sells as Lipitor. The second patent—which does cover the exact molecular form—should be invalidated, Ranbaxy has said, because it does not represent a real advance over the first patent."

The *Times* article made clear that the enantiomer patent in the U.S. expired after the basic patent.

* * *

Despite the mixed verdict in the U.K. decision, November ended on a good note.

On November 28 the U.S. Patent Office, despite its earlier rejection in June, reconfirmed our Lipitor crystalline patent.

Law360 carried the good news.

"In a significant victory for Pfizer, Inc., the U.S. Patent and Trademark Office is planning to issue a re-examination certificate for a contested patent for its best-selling drug, the $9.2 billion cholesterol fighter Lipitor."

However, as the New York Times' article had elaborated upon, the important decision in the U. S. had not yet arrived. For the remainder of the fall, we worked on all the other

Lipitor cases around the world and waited patiently for Judge Farnan's decision.

CHAPTER 12 – D-DAY
New York City, December 16, 2005

It had been over a year since the trial concluded, and we thought that Judge Farnan might issue his decision before he left for the Christmas holiday. December's days were clicking by, and our nerves were starting to fray.

Dinnertime. For a change, I was at home, if still on a conference call. My cell phone beeped; I ignored it. Only seconds later, the home phone rang in the next room. My antennae went up. While it was not unusual for me to get calls at any hour of the day or night, callers did not, as a rule, feel compelled to track me down all around the house. The conference call on my cell continued; the home phone kept ringing until my son, Chad, answered it.

"Just a minute, please," I heard him say.

With a worried look on his normally placid face, he brought the home phone to me.

"Mom, I think you better take this; it's about your Lipitor case."

I leapt up, and dumping the cell phone into the seat of my desk chair, I accepted the house phone from my son's outstretched hand. I took a breath before speaking. One. . . two. . . I didn't get to three.

It was Rudy delivering the news that Judge Farnan had just issued his decision.

We had won on both patents!

My mind went blank. This is what I'd hoped for, prayed for, for three very long, demanding years. My head started spinning. I couldn't move, speak, or respond in any way. Then. . . a well of emotions flooded inside me. I was dancing up and down on the spot and screaming into the phone between the steps of my own crazy jig. My first shriek startled my son who'd spun around to take in the sight, and my husband, Joel, appeared at his shoulder. A few seconds later, our daughter, Kyra, joined the startled onlookers. For a second or two, they might indeed have wondered if I was squealing in joy or anguish, but the look on my face—my wild-eyed excitement and a grin that couldn't stop—soon told them that we had won.

We had won.

Despite all the naysayers and doubting Thomases on Wall Street, we had won!

For three years, the Lipitor case had taken over my life. It had taken me away from my family and friends. My family and I might have suffered for it, but this win would protect thousands of jobs and the livelihoods of thousands of other families. Glorious as this moment was, I had no doubt that what Joel was thinking was that maybe now our family could at last get back to normal. It's what I was thinking, and hoping, too.

The story hit the front page of every major newspaper. The *New York Times* was among the dozens of national newspapers to carry the story on the front page of its business section.

"A federal judge yesterday rejected a patent challenge to Lipitor, a cholesterol-lowering medicine from Pfizer that is the world's top-selling drug.

The ruling was released after the 4:00 p.m. close of regular trading on the New York Stock Exchange. In after-hours trading, Pfizer's shares rose more than 11 percent.

Judge Joseph J. Farnan Jr. of Federal District Court in Delaware ruled that two crucial patents protecting atorvastatin, the active ingredient in Lipitor, are valid."

The *Times*, however, did not forgo the opportunity to also expound on the negative aspect of our win.

"The decision is crucial for Pfizer, which by some estimates makes as much as 30 percent of its profit from sales of Lipitor in the United States. The decision also means that patients and insurers will pay higher prices for atorvastatin (Lipitor) than if the patent had been invalidated. Prices for medicines can drop as much as 90 percent once they face generic competition."

The story chose to focus on Pfizer's ability, in light of the court's decision, to continue to charge higher prices for Lipitor. No one seemed to notice or care that the Lipitor patents were valid, but that we nevertheless had to prove that over and over again in various legal proceedings around the world. Or the fact that after three long years, our "win" only afforded us the right to keep what was lawfully ours to begin with.

Nevertheless, our celebrations were grand and numerous. Notes of congratulations poured in. Parties proliferated. Flowers arrived in profusion. Pfizer was king. We were the local heroes. The triumph of the moment bred optimism about the future.

It was our Hollywood moment.

But it was only that.

A moment.

Our brief foray into stardom was short-lived indeed.

CHAPTER 13 - UNEXPECTED LOSSES
New York City, April–August 2006

The spring started off on a good note and obscured, for a short while, the darkness that was soon to follow. I was sitting at my desk preparing for the upcoming appeal in the U.K. when Carol Williams walked into my office with a letter in her outstretched hand. *Now what*, I thought as I took it from her. I noticed the Hofstra University Law School letterhead and looked up at Carol so quickly that I snapped my neck out of place. Her face gave nothing away; she'd mastered the litigator's poker stare very well over the years. I didn't need to read far.

"The Admission Committee of Hofstra University Law School is pleased to offer you . . ."

What followed was lost to my tear-filled eyes. Jubilant, I tossed the acceptance letter into the air like a graduation cap that I hoped Carol would be wearing in three years. Carol Ann Williams, at the age of forty-seven, was going to law school.

YES!!

* * *

Kindler was named CEO on July 28, 2006. It was my brother in the ears-to-the-ground financial world who first told me the news. On the night of Friday, July 28, 2006, my cell phone rang.

"So, your man Kindler," he began.

"What now?"

"He's just been named CEO."

"Holy shit!"

I sank into a kitchen chair. It was very unusual for a Pfizer CEO to retire prior to his sixty-fifth birthday, and the most trusted ones stayed on for years afterward as advisors and members of the board. I had mixed emotions. On some level, I was happy for Kindler, but on another, more personal one, I was very sad for Hank.

The board placed the blame for Pfizer's lack of performance and declining stock price on Hank. Unfair as the judgment was, it was also a corporate truth that the buck stops at the desk of the CEO. Kindler was not entering the office without challenges.

Kindler's promotion lodged another concern for me, my team, and the whole legal division. Pfizer would be hiring a new general counsel, the third in less than four years. Yet, why should our group be different from any other division? Research had changed heads five times in five years, likewise HR. Such frequent changes in the company's executive structure marked a decided shift from the "family" I had joined in 1980, when it was not uncommon for a president, a general counsel, or an elevator operator to spend his or her entire career at Pfizer.

* * *

Kindler had barely settled into his CEO chair when the first in a series of unexpected and quite unfortunate setbacks for Pfizer befell us. Just five days later, on Wednesday, August 2, the Court of Appeals issued its decision in the Lipitor appeal. I had just returned from lunch.

The phone was ringing as I sat down at my desk.

It was Rudy. This time the news was not so favorable.

The court had upheld Judge Farnan's decision on the basic patent but overturned it on the enantiomer, holding a critical claim invalid on a technical defect in the way it had been drafted. It was sort of like saying that a sentence is invalid for bad grammar.

I put down the phone and retreated to the ladies' room. I splashed cold water on the face I no longer recognized. In the last few years, I had aged in a way I could not have predicted.

When I returned to my office, I didn't know what to do first—read the decision or call Kindler. I decided I'd better make the dreaded call before Kindler got the news from another source. I dialed his private cell phone number, the one to be used only in emergencies. I spat out the words as rapidly as possible, as if that would somehow lessen their impact.

Even though Hank was no longer CEO, I felt that he nonetheless deserved the courtesy of hearing about the decision from me. I placed the call to his office. As I waited for Hank to pick up the phone, my mind whirled back over all the wonderful moments I'd shared with him, all the kind words he'd given my group, all the encouragement and support he'd lent me over the years—his Crouching Tiger, Hidden Dragon—who usually won cases, not lost them. Hank had been very, very good to me. And now, on the eve of his departure, I'd had to deliver this bad news.

The story soon hit the electronic news wires, and the next day, it was the stuff of front-page headlines. Our stock took a hit along with our pride, falling 38 cents a share to $25.61. Our critics did the math. The *New York Times* was among the many newspapers to carry the story on August 3.

"Pfizer may face generic competition to its top-selling drug Lipitor a year earlier than analysts expected after a federal appeals court invalidated one of the company's patents. The Lipitor cholesterol pill had sales of $12.2 billion last year. Analysts had projected that the drug would not have competition from cheaper generic versions until June 2011. Pfizer projected last month that sales of Lipitor would reach $13 billion this year. 'If they lose 14 months, that's 14 months of lost revenue for Lipitor,' Anthony Butler, an analyst with Lehman Brothers in New York, said. 'On that assumption, the value would be about 35 cents a share.'"

Only the day before, the press had reported that Novo Nordisk had sued Pfizer claiming that our new inhaled-insulin product, Exubera, infringed its patents. Novo was thus seeking an injunction to stop us from selling what was, at the time, one of Pfizer's most promising new products.

Kindler had been at the helm for a mere five days.

* * *

When the dust settled, I read the CAFC decision. On page twelve, I noticed the following sentence: "We recognize that the patentee was attempting to claim what might otherwise have been patentable subject matter. Indeed, claim 6 could have been properly drafted either as dependent from claim 1 or as an independent claim."

The next day, Peter was quoted in the August 3 *New York Times'* article indicating that Pfizer would seek to correct this technical defect.

"Peter Richardson, Pfizer's associate general counsel, said the ruling was based on a 'technical defect' in the patent that the company would seek to change."

On August 11, Pfizer issued a similar statement in its 10-Q filing.

"The U.S. Patent and Trademark Office has a process for correcting technical defects in patents, and we plan to pursue that process with regard to our enantiomer patent."

The hope that we could correct the technical defect buoyed our spirits for a while.

* * *

Thankfully, the U.K. appeal proved to be a nonevent. We'd drawn a fair panel comprised of Justices Chadwick,

Jabob and Neuberger. The Justices indulged us on the first morning of the scheduled two day hearing. Simon presented our case, and the judges politely listened, at least for a few hours. Then, one of the justices rose and announced that they were going to take a short break. Ten minutes later, when they returned to the courtroom, they more or less told Simon not to proceed with his presentation any further because they were going to rule against us on the enantiomer patent. Fortunately, they did uphold Justice Pumfrey's decision on the basic patent.

It had not been a good summer for our team or for Pfizer. The fall, unfortunately, would show us how much worse things could get.

CHAPTER 14 - EUROPEAN MADNESS
New York City, September-December 2006

As Kindler was now CEO, he had to choose a new general counsel to replace himself. To no one's surprise, he chose Allen Waxman, whom a few years before, he'd brought into the company as head of the product liability litigation group. Waxman was not an IP attorney, but he was smart, he'd learn fast, and from the outset, he made every effort to understand our world. The *Wall Street Journal* reported on Waxman's approach to heading the legal affairs of Pfizer.

"Pfizer can't let lawsuits and the threat of litigation drive business decisions. 'We won't be able to avoid lawsuits, and considering the environment we face, we cannot even try to avoid them. The best we can do is make an honest effort to provide the best medical care we can, and to put ourselves in a position to handle those lawsuit when they come.'"

I liked Waxman's mindset. I was tired of being held hostage to generics and their never-ending attacks on Pfizer's patents. It reminded me of free shots on goal in a soccer match. The worst that could happen to you was that you did not score a point. The generics had nothing to lose by their patent challenges except the litigation fees. The situation was very different for the research-based company that was trying to protect the patents covering inventions that had taken decades and billions of dollars to procure.

* * *

We were deep into the international Lipitor cases when Waxman took over, but he got up to speed quickly. It was not an easy task. By fall, we had Lipitor cases pending in the U.S., Canada, all the major Asian markets, and every single European country, except, strangely enough, France.

We'd had other notable French cases over the years though. In particular, two earlier well-known ones. In the first case, in the early 1990s, Pfizer brought a suit against the French pharmaceutical company, Sarget-Plantier, over the patent for the old antibiotic product, doxycycline, the drug of choice to treat respiratory infections before azithromycin hit the market. The case went all the way up to the highest French Court, the Cour de Cassation, where Pfizer won.

The second, more notorious case in France concerned the Viagra trademark. We were about to launch Viagra in Europe when Dr. Virag, a well-known specialist in the male erectile dysfunction area, filed a suit against Pfizer and requested a preliminary injunction, claiming that we had used his name in choosing the Viagra trademark. Viagra, he alleged, was an anagram of Virag.

It wasn't true.

The Viagra trademark, now attached to the drug sildenafil for treatment of erectile dysfunction, had been intended for another Pfizer drug that was being developed to treat male urinary problems. The name Viagra, in fact, had evolved from that of Niagra, a play on Niagara, as in the falls, which was meant to suggest a steady stream. The "N" was then changed to a "V" so as to convey the idea of vitality or virility. The urinary drug, however, had never made it to market, and the Viagra trademark was shelved for possible future use. Nevertheless, Dr. Virag had insisted that the celebrated trademark had originated in his name.

* * *

On our arrival in Paris, we'd checked into our favorite hotel and then had set off to meet with Dr. Virag and his team. Despite the fact that he was fluent in English, Dr. Virag spoke in French to the group at large and switched to English only when he was addressing Peter and me. It was a big mistake: Peter and I are fluent in French. So we were happy to allow the doctor his language and followed his every word.

Thus, when Dr. Virag had proposed a settlement, we had politely declined. The verifiable fact that Pfizer had not usurped his name in the selection of the Viagra trademark won the day in court.

Although the break we got on Lipitor in France was not insignificant, litigation in all the other European countries still remained in play. The typical 9:00 a.m. decision in Europe meant, for the most part, that we'd have to get up at 3:00 a.m. in New York to await it. To stay awake and alert until the news of the decisions arrived, we text-messaged each other jokes.

We'd won on the basic patent in most of the major European countries at this point, hence Ranbaxy was enjoined from selling their copycat product in those markets. However, Ranbaxy had launched at-risk in Denmark, without waiting for the judge's decision. We asked for a preliminary injunction as well as a recall of the Ranbaxy product, and the following February Justice Larsen granted Pfizer's request. Ranbaxy had to withdraw its product. News Medical carried the story.

"The injunction, issued by the Bailiff's Court of the Copenhagen City Court in Denmark and subject to possible appeal by Nomeco, requires Ranbaxy's generic atorvastatin product to be withdrawn from the Danish market pending the outcome of a patent infringement trial that has not yet been scheduled.

At issue are three Pfizer patents covering atorvastatin calcium, the active ingredient in Lipitor, as well as processes and intermediate compounds used to make atorvastatin. The latest-expiring of the patents provides coverage for Lipitor through November, 2011. The Bailiff's Court ruled in Pfizer's favor on all three patents. 'This ruling is another significant milestone in our defense of Lipitor patents around the world,' said Pfizer Senior Vice President and General Counsel Allen Waxman. 'And it's an important outcome for Pfizer and other medical innovators who invest in high-risk research to develop life-saving medicines for millions of patients,' added Karin Verland, country manager of Denmark."

We didn't have much time to celebrate any of our victories, however, because Pfizer would soon face one of its biggest setbacks in years.

* * *

In the first week of December, Pfizer announced that it had discontinued research on our most promising candidate in the company's pipeline—torcetrapib, the cholesterol-lowering compound to replace Lipitor. The major setback was covered in every major newspaper. The *New York Times* summed it up in a succinct article.

"Pfizer announced last night that it had discontinued research on its most important experimental drug, a treatment for heart disease. The decision is a stunning development that is likely to seriously damage the company's prospects through the next decades."

The losses, though, went far and beyond the millions of developmental dollars and the billions in unrealized future revenue. The biggest losers of all were the heart patients now denied the promise of a new, more effective cholesterol-lowering drug, as the *New York Times* headline the following day made clear:

"End of Drug Trial is a Big Loss for Pfizer and Heart Patients."

The *Times* elaborated on the disappointing news.

"The news came to Pfizer's chief scientist, Dr. John L. LaMattina, as he was showering at 7:00 a.m. Saturday: the company's most promising experimental drug, intended to treat heart disease, actually caused an increase in deaths and heart problems. Eighty-two people had died so far in a clinical trial, versus 51 people in the same trial who had not taken it.

Within hours, Pfizer, the world's largest drug maker, told more than 100 trial investigators to stop giving patients the drug, called torcetrapib. Shortly after 9:00 a.m. Saturday, Pfizer announced that it had pulled the plug on the medicine entirely, turning the company's nearly $1 billion investment in it into a total loss.

The abrupt decision to discontinue torcetrapib was a shocking disappointment for Pfizer and for people who suffer from heart disease. The drug, which has been in development since the early 1990s, raises so-called good cholesterol and cardiologists had hoped it would reduce the buildup of plaques in blood vessels that can cause heart attacks. Just last Thursday, Pfizer's chief executive, Jeffrey B. Kindler, said publicly that the drug could be among the most important new developments for heart disease in decades and that the company hoped to get Food and Drug Administration approval for it in 2007."

The last five months had not been good ones: We had lost the enantiomer patent, we'd been sued by Novo Nordisk, and now we had lost our biggest and most promising new drug candidate. But mercifully, as 2006 drew to an end, I did not know that 2007 would herald a personal crisis for me far more devastating than the sum total of all the professional disappointments of 2006 combined.

CHAPTER 15 - A BROOKLYN TALE
New York City, January 2007

The roar of the crowd no doubt carried far beyond the four streets that served as the boundaries for the first American baseball park to be enclosed by a fence. Baseball's first paying customers had been streaming into Union Grounds all morning. The inaugural match, played on May 15, 1862, drew residents from their homes and occupants from their businesses on the northeastern side of the park—along Harrison Avenue in the heart of Williamsburg, Brooklyn— into the throng.

A few blocks down Harrison, at the corner of Bartlett Street, Charles Erhart and his German American cousin, Charles Pfizer, left their premises and ventured out onto the street to join in the excitement. The fine chemicals business the two cousins had started thirteen years earlier had met with resounding success. They, too, had had an opening day of sorts to celebrate in 1862. That year saw Pfizer's first domestic production of tartaric acid and cream of tartar, products that would soon become vital to the food and the chemical industries.

Union Grounds did not survive long. It was demolished in 1883. But Pfizer thrived. By the 1880s, the company had started producing citric acid, which brought national recognition to the cousins and their business. Six decades later, with the outbreak of World War II, the company began its march toward its status as the largest pharmaceutical company in the world. The war called for unprecedented amounts of penicillin, and the U.S. government turned to Pfizer to produce it.

The Brooklyn plant, still operating at Harrison Avenue and Bartlett Street, was among the first plants to close. It was extensively covered in the press, but the *New York Times* carried an especially poignant, as well as an understanding article.

"If this area on the Williamsburg—Bedford-Stuyvesant border is not quite Pfizerville, it still may be the closest thing to a factory town in this largely postindustrial city. For 158 years, the Pfizer company has presided over this remote-feeling stretch of Brooklyn, a windswept, big-sky place sliced like a pie by broad, angling streets: first as industrial magnet, then a big brother-benefactor. So Pfizer's imminent departure, which the company announced on Monday, will mean more than the loss of 600 jobs.

On Monday, Pfizer, the world's biggest pharmaceutical firm, said it would slash 7,800 jobs in the United States, Europe and Japan. Several of its best-selling drugs are losing their patent protection and will face competition from cheaper generics.

In many quarters, the announcement was not exactly surprising. For a while now, continuing to operate the Brooklyn plant, where Lipitor, Zoloft, Viagra and other drugs are manufactured and distributed, seemed more a good-will gesture to the borough of Pfizer's birth than a business decision."

Kindler soon announced the closure of several other research sites, including Ann Arbor where Bruce Roth worked. He attempted to explain the decision in the media.

"Pfizer is a great company with a great future. We are facing significant challenges, however, in a profoundly changing business environment. I believe we must fundamentally change the way we run our company and meet these challenges to take advantage of the diverse and attractive opportunities we see in the marketplace."

When our Ann Arbor research site closed, Bruce Roth, the inventor of Lipitor, was out of a job. Roth first synthesized Lipitor in 1985 and had received the 1997 Warner-Lambert Chairman's Distinguished Scientific Achievement Award, the 1999 Inventor of the Year Award from the New York Intellectual Property Law Association, the 2003 American Chemical Society Award for Creative Invention, the 2003 Gustavus John Esselen Award for Chemistry in the Public Service, the 2005 Iowa State University Distinguished Alumni Award, and the 2006 Pfizer Global Research and Development Achievement Award. He'd been named a 2008 Hero of Chemistry by the American Chemical Society (ACS). In addition, Roth was the designated inventor or co-inventor on forty-two patents other than Lipitor.

* * *

Despite the plant closures, continual mergers and acquisitions would soon make Pfizer a conglomerate of what had once been more than a dozen freestanding pharmaceutical companies, including other household names such as Searle, Parke Davis, Upjohn, American Cyanamid, and American Home Products.

Pfizer adopted a slogan, "The Spirit of Small, the Power of Scale" that Kindler had used to explain the goal of the enormous company we had become. One such explanation had appeared in the August 2, 2006 edition of *Pharmaceutical Executive*.

"A few years ago, we adopted a slogan for my division: The Spirit of Small, the Power of Scale. And our logo shows a bunch of tiny little fish all moving in the same direction, and then the tiny little fish start to merge and they become a giant whale. We want to try, to the extent that we can in this large an organization to have the spirit of a small company."

People's opinions were divided on whether this was possible. One of Pfizer's former heads of research, John LaMattina, has written extensively about the changes in the pharmaceutical industry. In the August 2011 issue of *Nature Reviews/Drug Discovery*, he opines on the impact mergers have had on pharmaceutical research. He sums up their effect with one word: "devastating."

"In this article, it is argued that although mergers and acquisitions in the pharmaceutical industry might have had a reasonable short-term business rationale, their impact on the R&D of the organizations involved has been devastating."

In the December 2012 issue of *Forbes* magazine LaMattina discusses specific effects of research turmoil on the development time of new drugs. In the article, he focuses on a promising breast cancer treatment, PD-332,991.

"As I have stated in the past, major mergers take a toll on a company in many ways, particularly morale and productivity. PD-332,991 seems to have been a victim of such a scenario. This compound was nominated for development in Pfizer in 2002 and. . . languished in phase 1 until January, 2010, when it finally advanced to phase 2. It normally only takes 12 months for a compound to proceed through phase 1 studies. Why did this compound lag in phase 1 for six years?"

LaMattina is by no means alone in exploring the adverse effects of corporate mergers. Bruce Booth, in an April 2012 article appearing in Forbes, postulates that culture—a culture of change—is the culprit in the current R&D crisis:

"These [changes] cause constant organizational upheaval with levels of distraction that can't be measured. Resumes fly through cyberspace as soon as a deal is announced. Organizations are frozen as these changes happen, fear of the unknown paralyzes entire project teams, and closures/layoffs happen without much regard to upgrading the talent and weeding out the deadwood."

But in 2007 the effect of mergers had not yet been fully considered, much less understood. Hindsight is indeed always

20/20. At the time, mergers were believed to be necessary, if not essential, to the industry's survival.

The cost-reduction programs were given benign names, such as *Adapting to Scale*, but Pfizer was cutting back, and everyone knew it. The press was all over it, quoting Kindler's own words when reporting on the company's third quarter results.

"As a critical step in our transformation, we are taking a comprehensive look at our costs, and in 2007 we plan to implement a new company-wide cost-reduction initiative that will lower our cost base in 2007 and 2008 as well as give us greater flexibility to modulate our expenses in the face of changing market conditions. These savings will be over and above the $4 billion projected annual cost savings by 2008 from our *Adapting to Scale* (AtS) productivity initiative."

Of course, we needed to be proactive—needed to meet the challenges posed by a rapidly changing industry, as Kindler had averred—and, more important, we had to be *seen* by Wall Street to be taking decisive action.

CHAPTER 16 - THE LONGEST WINTER
New York City, April 16, 2007

Spring was slow in coming in 2007. It was mid-April, and New York was still cold—it had snowed again. All the eastern states were experiencing it. Even Virginia, normally warm by now, had had a snowfall that fateful mid-April morning.

We had lost our Canadian case at trial in January, and our important appeal was just over a month away. We'd arranged a two-day meeting in New York to prepare for it with our Canadian attorneys, Peter Wilcox and Andrew Shaughnessy who had arrived earlier that morning. Everyone was assembling in the conference room to hear their presentation when the first news alert flickered across my computer monitor.

Shooter.

Virginia Tech.

I stopped short, sat back down at my desk, and in five seconds, I had my brother, Jeff, on the phone.

"What's going on at Tech?"

"I don't know. Apparently there is a shooter on campus."

"Have they caught him yet?"

"No."

I dropped the desk phone. Frantic, I picked up my cell and called my daughter, Kyra. She was a sophomore at Virginia Tech.

No answer.

I called again.

No answer.

I called Jeff back.

"Do you know anything else?"

"The campus is on lockdown now. Apparently the shooter killed a girl in the Ambler Johnson dorm around seven this morning."

"So it's a lover's spat?"

"I don't think so, Sis."

Again I called Kyra. I was thankful she didn't live near the Ambler Johnson dorm. Still, my heart was pounding, my palms were sweating, and my mouth was dry.

No answer.

"Come on, Kyra, pick up!" I shouted at the phone.

My assistant appeared in my office door.

"They're waiting for you in the conference room, Traci."

"Tell them to start without me, please. There's been a shooting at Virginia Tech."

"Isn't that where you went to college?"

"Yes, I did, and that is where Kyra's in college now."

There was an audible gasp from my doorway, and my assistant disappeared.

Another frantic call to Kyra. No answer. Click. Redial. No answer. Click. Redial. No answer.

I was silently screaming.

"Please, God, no. Not Kyra."

My assistant again appeared in my doorway.

"They're starting."

"I can't join them until I hear Kyra's voice."

Another redial.

"Hello."

The voice was weak, but it was Kyra's! Desperate as I'd been to hear it, to hear her, it took me by surprise. I was switching the phone from my left hand to my right and dropped it on the floor. I tried to gather my composure. I knelt down, retrieved the phone, and sat sprawled, unladylike, across the floor. At least I'd worn pants to work that day.

"You okay, sweetie?"

Soft sobbing.

"I'm okay, Mom."

"Please don't leave your apartment."

"Don't worry, Mom; the campus is on lockdown now."

We finished talking; I was reassured that Kyra was safe. Then I called my brother again.

"Kyra is okay. Have they caught the shooter yet?"

"I don't think so, but the reports are slow and conflicting, so I'm really not sure."

"I have to go into a meeting for the rest of the morning, but I will put my BlackBerry on the table on silent. Please send me any updates you get."

* * *

Still shaken, I joined my team and the visiting attorneys in the conference room.

"I'm sorry to be late, but there's been a shooting at my daughter's school in Virginia, and I was trying to reach her to make sure she was okay."

"Oh my God," exclaimed Will. "Was anyone killed?"

"Yes."

"How many?"

"They've reported three so far. It may be some sort of lover's quarrel, but no one knows yet."

I sat through the morning prep session half in a trance. My thoughts were disjointed.

Patents.

Shooter.

Case law.

Murder.

We broke for lunch and headed across the street to The Capitol Grille, where we had a noon reservation. At the table, the discussion focused on critical points of the morning presentation, but my mind and eyes attended only to my BlackBerry as I watched and waited for updates from my brother, himself a Virginia Tech alumnus. Halfway through the first course, an update arrived at last.

"Casualty list is now 16."

Thirty minutes later, another update.

"Casualty list now at 28 but expected to rise."

At last came the email telling me the rampage had ended.

"The shooter is dead."

My audible sigh of relief gave way to unexpected tears.

Will glanced in my direction. The last three years had taken their emotional toll, and I could see genuine concern on his face. I excused myself and retreated to the ladies' room.

* * *

Before the long afternoon prep session, I turned on the TV in my office and hit the record button so I could watch the news later. At 7:00 p.m. everyone headed off to dinner; I promised to join them in thirty minutes. Back in my office, I hit the rewind button and started fast-forwarding through the day's news coverage.

Chaos.

Paramedics were carrying a girl on a stretcher outside of Norris Hall, where most of the students had been shot. The girl was wearing a white T-shirt and jeans.

My breath caught in my throat. I hit the rewind button and then zoomed in on her face. Again I rewound the tape. I zoomed in even closer.

The girl, I was certain, was one of Kyra's friends. In the frame on the TV screen, she appeared to be alive, but I couldn't be sure. I wondered if Kyra knew, and I felt a familiar mixture of relief and guilt—guilt in my relief that Kyra was okay when many other students were not.

Thirty-two. In the end, that's what the dead numbered, plus the gunman himself. Thirty-two names, thirty-two lives cut short with histories too brief: Ross A. Alameddine, Christopher James Bishop, Brian R. Bluhm, Ryan Christopher Clark, Austin Michelle Cloyd, Jocelyne Couture-Nowak, Kevin P. Granata, Matthew Gregory Gwaltney, Caitlin Millar Hammaren, Jeremy Michael Herbstritt, Rachael Elizabeth Hill, Emily Jane Hilscher, Jarrett Lee Lane, Matthew Joseph La Porte, Henry J. Lee, Liviu Librescu, G. V. Loganathan, Partahi Mamora Halomoan Lumbantoruan, Lauren Ashley McCain, Daniel Patrick O'Neil, Juan Ramon Ortiz-Ortiz, Minal Hiralal Panchal, Daniel Alejandro Perez Cueva, Erin Nicole Peterson, Michael Steven Pohle Jr., Julia Kathleen Pryde, Mary Karen Read, Reema Joseph Samaha, Waleed Mohamed Shaalan, Leslie Geraldine Sherman, Maxine Shelly Turner, and Nicole Regina White.

Numerous others suffered serious injury, among them Kyra's friend, who'd spend many months in the hospital fighting for her young life. She'd be counted as one of the "lucky ones" who had escaped the slaughter in Norris Hall that tragic Monday morning.

It was the deadliest shooting by a single gunman in U.S. history during a time of peace.

* * *

A few days later, Virginia Tech held a memorial service in the coliseum. It concluded with the university president's counsel to the student body: "Go to where you are safe and loved."

The next day, Kyra flew home. Joel and I were waiting for her by the luggage carousel at LaGuardia, where we heard the announcement over the loudspeaker.

"Flight 4204 from Roanoke has landed."

Other parents were waiting there as well, in silence. We all shared the same stunned look that combined shock and grief with tired-eyed relief.

Our children were alive.

First to emerge from the plane were the newscasters who had been covering the tragedy in Blacksburg, but my interest was fixed only on Kyra that morning. The first student to come down the steps from the plane was impossible to miss. She was wearing a Virginia Tech T-shirt. But it was the haunted look on her pale face that told the real story. Then another student, another college T-shirt, another haunted look. And another.

It was clear these kids were traumatized.

Finally Kyra appeared, she too in a Virginia Tech shirt. Her eyes almost swollen shut from crying, she fell into my arms. Her knees buckled beneath her. I held her up. It had been a long time since I'd held the entire weight of her thin body in my arms. I spoke as quickly as I could find words—any words—to say. I settled for a few short sentences of assurance.

"It will be okay. It will be okay. You will get through this."

She didn't reply.

I took her home, bathed her, and put her to bed. She slept for the rest of the day. I meanwhile worked at my laptop on the Canadian case. My daughter entered crisis counseling. As she struggled to come to terms with an inexplicable tragedy, I tried to focus both on her needs and on Pfizer's. As for my own needs, I had increasingly less time to attend to them, or even any inclination to acknowledge them.

CHAPTER 17 - O CANADA
Ontario, May 2007-March 2008

On May 22, 2007 we set off for the appellate hearing in Ottawa. I was expecting at least a nip in the air, given winter's overextended visit up and down the eastern seaboard that year, but on disembarking, we stepped into an early summer. Ottawa was Hottawa, and Hottawa was a pleasant, welcome surprise.

A beautiful, clean city built on the river from which it takes its name, Ottawa offers the charms and startling appositions of a European city. Its quaint old passageways and new high-rise glass towers create a dramatic view. One moment, you're standing in a modern, air-conditioned courthouse, and the next you're walking down a cobblestone street two centuries back in time. By day we attended the appellate hearing, but by night we allowed ourselves a few hours off to enjoy a meal in one of the outdoor cafes that had been quickly assembled to take advantage of the unexpected, glorious weather.

* * *

We had drawn the three-member appellate panel consisting of Justices Linden, Nadon, and Ryer. The courtroom was somber and serious and tension soon mounted. Will, who's quite a hand at the sketch pad, had taken to drawing silly caricatures of us during the first trial before Judge Farnan to lighten the mood. His pen was busy again at the appellate hearing in Canada.

"Here, look at this. Guess who?"

He handed me a sketch of the two of us sitting in the courtroom, our eyes glued to the three judges in front of us. I had to bury my face, and laughter, in my lap or risk being asked to leave the courtroom for inappropriate behavior. Will had accomplished his purpose; he'd brought a welcome, if brief, respite from the courtroom's mounting tension.

The two days allotted for the hearing were nearing an end, and the time for closing arguments arrived. We used every last second to make sure the three judges understood how extraordinary it was for the Lipitor molecule to have ever been discovered in the first place. Our Canadian counsel were terrific.

Exhausted but optimistic, we headed back to New York.

Fortunately, we had no idea what would be waiting for us there.

And when the dust settled from the latest explosion in our world, figuratively and literally, our lives were shattered in a way none of us could have predicted.

* * *

July 18, 2007: A bomb exploded.

A terrorist attack, like 9/11, we were sure. Only it was not in the heart of the financial district. This time, it had hit in the heart of midtown.

In fact, right outside our office windows.

Or what was left of them.

At the exact moment of the explosion one of my colleagues was sitting at his desk when a sound like thunder filled his ears. The next second, he was blown out of his seat.

Literally.

Our first thoughts placed the target at Grand Central Station across the street. All of us were unnerved, but Will was so shaken that he ran out of the building and thirty blocks up Third Avenue before he stopped.

Eventually we learned that a steam pipe, not a terrorist device, had exploded on Lexington Avenue. It was just past 8:00 p.m. when Mayor Bloomberg stepped into position at a bank of microphones. Cameras were whirring. Videotape was rolling. The mayor looked somber:

"This evening at about 5:57, a call came in for an explosion on 41st and Lexington. There is no reason to believe whatsoever that this is anything other than a failure of our infrastructure. A steam pipe, twenty-four inches in diameter, installed in 1924, burst. It may have burst because of cold water from the rain, it may have burst because of a water-main break that we don't know about yet, but in any case, the steam pipe broke and that's what you've seen. At the moment, the steam has been turned off and there's no more vapor coming out of the hole. In terms of injuries, sadly we believe—and the numbers may change through the evening—that one person died from cardiac arrest and that person we believe to be at Bellevue Hospital."

One person had indeed had a heart attack. And of all the people who were in New York City that day, that one person was a Pfizer legal division colleague. The death of Lois Baumerich brought the explosion and its effects very close to home for us as had the deaths of two Pfizer colleagues killed during 9/11: Jean Collins and Joseph DeLuca.

* * *

The trauma following the explosion subsided. Once the shattered glass had been picked up and the debris cleared, so too, did our heads clear and moods pick up.

In August, our wonderful new chief financial officer, Frank D'Amelio, arrived to replace David Shedlarz, who had retired after Kindler was named CEO. Smart and incisive though he was, Frank was not your standard Harvard-educated man but rather more of a rough-and-tumble street guy who'd worked his way up the corporate ladder the old-fashioned way—by sheer, raw intelligence, guts, determination, and hard work. He was not afraid to make a tough decision or to stick to it once it was made. He looked the part, too: Italian, with rugged good looks; and his sleeves rolled up, as if he was always ready for business. Which he was.

* * *

We were not able to be happy about our new CFO for very long, however. On August 16, 2007 we received the news that our request to have the enantiomer patent reissued, following the correction of the technical defect, had been denied. The *Wall Street Journal* was among the many newspapers to herald the story. The headline spoke for itself.

"Pfizer's Lipitor Patent Reissue Rejected."

While not good news, an initial rejection is not uncommon as the text of the article made clear.

"The U. S. Patent and Trademark Office has preliminarily rejected Pfizer Inc.'s request for the reissue of a patent for its Lipitor cholesterol drug that would preserve its U.S. market exclusivity until 2011, the agency's Web site indicated.

The Lipitor patent was invalidated last year by a federal appeals court after it was challenged by Ranbaxy Laboratories Ltd., an Indian generic-drug company that wants to sell a copycat version of Lipitor. A second patent was upheld, preserving Pfizer's U.S. market exclusivity for Lipitor until March 2010.

New York-based Pfizer applied to the patent office in January to have the 2011 patent reissued, and to correct a "technical defect" in the original patent. A reissue would extend Pfizer's market exclusivity through June 2011.

But the patent office listed on its Web site Wednesday a "non-final rejection" of Pfizer's request for a patent reissue, though it didn't link any documents explaining its action. The Web site also indicates a rejection letter was mailed to Pfizer Thursday.

A Pfizer spokesman said Thursday the company is awaiting a letter from the patent office explaining the decision. Because it's not a final rejection, Pfizer still has an opportunity to persuade the patent office to reissue the patent.

Lipitor is the best-selling drug in the world, with $12.9 billion in sales last year. However, it has faced pressure not only from ongoing patent challenges worldwide, but also from competition from generic versions of other anti-cholesterol drugs."

My team and I spent the last quarter of 2007 as we'd spent the one before, and the one before that. We continued working on the numerous Lipitor cases around the world.

And we waited for news from Canada.

* * *

The long-awaited Canadian appellate decision arrived the following March and gave us some breathing room.

We had won!

Peter had his typical understated reaction when I delivered the good news.

"No one ever said this business is easy."

It started 2008 off on a good note. I sent out a short note announcing the news.

Bloomberg was a bit more expansive in its press release and quoted Peter, as well.

"Pfizer Inc., the world's biggest drugmaker, won a Canadian appeals court ruling blocking regulatory approval of Ranbaxy Laboratories Ltd.'s generic version of the cholesterol pill Lipitor. Canada's Federal Court of Appeal yesterday reversed a lower-court ruling that Ranbaxy could seek approval for its competing version of Lipitor before Pfizer's patent expires in 2010, Pfizer spokeswoman Vanessa Aristide said in a phone interview.

Ranbaxy, India's largest drugmaker, also challenged Lipitor patents in the Netherlands. Pfizer said in February it would appeal a Dutch ruling invalidating one of its patents covering Lipitor, the world's best-selling medicine with sales of $12.7 billion last year. Ranbaxy can appeal yesterday's ruling to Canada's Supreme Court. The order doesn't apply to litigation in other countries, including the U.S. Aristide said.

The order affirms intellectual property rights in Canada and 'provides the incentive for research-driven pharmaceutical companies to make the significant high-risk investments,' Pfizer Associate General Counsel Peter Richardson said in a statement."

The win, however, was soon to prove to be the only good thing that happened that March.

CHAPTER 18 - THE IDES OF MARCH
New York City, March 2008

March 2008 changed my life forever. Other than the Canadian appellate win, things were going downhill. . . and fast. Any one of the three unfortunate events that occurred that month would have done it. All three of them in less than thirty days made it absolutely sure.

The stress of work was mounting.

In an effort to calm my nerves, I started swimming every morning in a swim machine, the swimmer's version of a treadmill.

Faster and faster.

Harder and harder.

Pounding away at the water, unloading my frustrations into it, I'd review the court cases in my mind, analyze them, and consider alternatives to our strategies and arguments to reassure myself we had done everything we could and done it right. Not only was I battling the whirling water, I was grappling with the Lipitor case at the same time.

My routine was interrupted one morning when the pool's endless current abruptly stopped. Through my fog-filled goggles, I looked up at my husband, hovering above me. He looked worried.

"You're going to hurt yourself if you don't slow it down a bit."

"I'm fine," I replied, barely hiding my aggravation.

Less with a smile than a grimace, I readjusted my goggles and hit the on button with a slap of my hand, as if to say I knew what I was doing, and plunged back into the cool water.

A few minutes later, I felt a snap in my right shoulder, and then a searing pain shot through my entire body. I was trying to stand up when I felt another, lesser snap, this one in my left arm.

I'd been swimming, then I wasn't, and couldn't.

My right arm hung limp at my side. I discounted the possibility that I might have had a stroke, and despite the intense, if localized pain, I got out of the pool, got dressed, and headed off to work. I had no choice. Time constraints allowed for no sick days or even momentary breaks to seek help.

* * *

My packed schedule that week was made all the more demanding because Peter was in Boston at another off-site meeting with some of our other legal division leaders. I'd had a wall-to-wall morning and was running late. I sprinted over to Grand Central to meet one of our outside counsel for lunch at Metrazur. Overwhelming though the importance of the Lipitor matter was, other major cases also fell under our responsibility, not the least of which was the pending Celebrex case, which was soon to go to trial in the U.S. As I had been waiting all morning for a call from Rudy about the status of the enantiomer reissue, I made an exception to my normal rule and set my cell phone on the table.

Our meals arrived and so did a phone call. Only it wasn't Rudy. It was Peter calling from Boston. My antennae rose. As the whole purpose of an off-site is to escape daily contact with the office, why was he calling?

"Excuse me one minute," I said to my lunch partner. "It's Peter, and I should take this."

"What's up?" I asked.

"Are you alone?" Peter asked.

Strange opening.

"No, why? What's wrong?" I asked, now focused on my phone.

"Where are you?"

"At Metrazur, discussing the Celebrex case."

"Okay, I'm going to tell you something, but you must not react or say anything."

Metrazur, a restaurant so elegant you'd think Grand Central might have been designed for it, sat at the top of a sweeping marble staircase and overlooked the main concourse. But, like the concourse itself, it was a very open space. I looked around and spotted a private area behind the bar. I waved my finger to indicate to my lunch partner that I'd be just a minute and walked away.

"Okay, what's up?"

"Waxman just quit!"

"What? Why?"

Peter told me what he knew, which wasn't much. Allen Waxman, our recently appointed general counsel, had showed up in Boston for the off-site but then told everyone that he had resigned, so no one was sure why he was even there.

No notice.

No explanation.

He'd simply quit. I started walking back to my table, my best litigator's poker face in place.

"Okay. Thanks for letting me know," I said to Peter and hung up.

I tried not to be distracted from my Celebrex conversation. Needless to say, I was.

"Everything okay?" asked my lunch partner.

No! Everything was not okay.

* * *

I'd scarcely returned to my office when Will came bursting in.

"Hey, did you hear that Waxman just resigned?"

"Yes, Peter called from Boston with the news but told me not to tell anyone," I replied. "Who told you?"

"Everyone knows," replied Will with a shrug.

I shouldn't have been surprised. It was not the type of news that could be kept secret for long.

"What do you think could be going on?" Will asked.

"No clue," I answered.

I could not even begin to imagine why Waxman would have quit, much less so without any notice at all. But, it didn't take long for the rumor mill to swing into high gear, and the pharmaceutical blogs were quick to speculate on what lay behind his sudden resignation.

The next day, Waxman called me.

"Hey, I just want to say goodbye and thank you for all you did to help me while I was here."

I could think of only one thing to say.

"Are you okay? Are you sick?"

"I just need to take a step back," he replied.

It wasn't much of an explanation, but I didn't think it was any of my business to press him further. I liked Waxman and was sorry to see him leave.

"Well, good luck; I hope everything will work out well for you," I said instead.

Waxman was gone. We'd soon be getting another general counsel.

* * *

That night I had a dream about Lipitor, a dream that would in time prove to be life-altering both professionally and personally. If I had known its far-reaching consequences, I may have chosen to ignore it.

But, alas, I didn't.

It was one of those dreams in which you seem to be vacillating eerily between a state of sleep and a waking reality in which you're thinking you're awake while at the same time thinking you are dreaming. The dream lit my bedroom in a yellowish sepia color, like an old photograph. I could hear a radio crackling in the distance, and fragments of war reports wafted off and on through the air: "Allied forces . . ." and then unintelligible mutterings. The warm morning air was gently blowing through my open bedroom window, and with it came a strange voice. I sat up in bed and listened. And in that instant I knew exactly what to do.

It seemed so perfect, and so simple. Then . . .

I was awake. My bedroom was dark. No radio was playing. The shades and curtains were drawn against the cold; a chill lingered in the winter air. I wondered if I was getting sick brought on by the unremitting stress of work and the burden of the responsibility that rested on my now very injured shoulders—the constant searing pain had become my new normal.

I called Peter. He was not happy to be awakened.

"Why are you calling me so early? I'm still in bed."

"Listen," I said, "and before you say anything, let me finish my story please."

I told him about my dream and the idea that had come to me in it. After a long pause, Peter said, "Let me get a cup of coffee and clear my head, and I'll call you back later."

As it turned out, I had little time to dwell on the dream.

CHAPTER 19 - LOST INNOCENCE
New York City, March – April 2008

Despite all the changes, Peter and I tried to keep everyone focused on work. We were starting to get our bearings when more unwelcome news hit us from the Patent Office. Our request for reissue of the enantiomer patent had been rejected for a second time. *Law360* was among the many sources to carry the news.

"The U. S. Patent and Trademark Office has again rebuffed Pfizer Inc.'s bid to reissue one of the patents behind its blockbuster cholesterol drug Lipitor. Pfizer disclosed Friday that the agency had issued its second preliminary rejection of U.S. Patent Number 5,273,995 marking a further setback in the pharmaceutical giant's quest to extend its U.S. market exclusivity for Lipitor until June 2011.

'Pfizer has received a second official action issued by the U.S. Patent & Trademark Office in response to its application to reissue the '995 enantiomer patent for atorvastatin calcium, the active ingredient for Lipitor,' the drugmaker said. 'Pfizer will now review the communication from the Patent Office and respond as appropriate to address the issues raised by the examiner.'

Pfizer was quick to point out that a second office action is not unusual in reissue applications and that it remains confident that the company will be able to address the examiner's issues.

'Reissue proceedings can involve complex issues, and the average time for obtaining a reissue patent is about two years from the time the application was filed,' the drugmaker said, while noting that the reissue application was only first filed in January 2007.

Even with the preliminary rejection, however, Pfizer observed that its Lipitor patents will still be protected for years to come.

'It is important to note, however, that Lipitor continues to be protected by its basic patent until March 2010, including pediatric exclusivity,' Pfizer said. 'Today's action has no impact on the basic patent.'

Pfizer has been fighting off attempts from generics makers to horn in on the market for its blockbuster drug in various courts in the U.S. and around the globe."

As the news article made clear, we could still attempt to reply to the examiner's latest round of objections, and we did.

* * *

Despite the fact that almost a year had passed since the Virginia Tech tragedy, I found it difficult to regain my bearings. The stress of work, coupled with my ever-worsening physical condition, was burden enough. But the Virginia Tech shooting, and the accompanying concern about Kyra's well-being, had sort of pushed me over the edge.

The childhood secret that I had suppressed was now working its way through the cracks in my carefully sealed memory. I grew up in a place and time when to "spare the rod and spoil the child" was a well-regarded axiom, and I know I was not the only kid in my neighborhood to have received a good whipping now and again. Nevertheless, child abuse is child abuse, and it has long-term negative consequences.

For the past twenty-five years I'd hidden my story, but sitting in my office one day thinking about the upcoming April 16 Virginia Tech "anniversary," it resurfaced from my unconscious memory.

* * *

It was in a quiet little neighborhood where all the houses were identical, at least on the outside, in a corner of my bedroom, out of sight, out of earshot of the neighbors, that a dark secret—a secret guarded for years, for decades—was seeded and bred. There, the toughness, the resilience, and even the will to win against all odds were beaten into me at the end of a slashing leather belt. Perhaps, in retrospect, my Crouching Tiger, Hidden Dragon moniker was really earned that fateful day. But no one knew my story. I had spared everyone my secret.

I was twelve years old. Later that day, I would be swimming in a relay event, the very one in which I would false start. The day began as had too many others. I'd endured it bravely; I'd had practice. Only that morning, after I'd had my whipping, after I'd wiped away the snot pouring from my nose, something inside me snapped as I'd watched my brother, Jeff, huddled in the corner crying, waiting for his turn. I, or the Crouching Tiger that had been born decades before Hank McKinnell unwittingly gave me that nickname, pounced. When I'd landed, I was straddling my mother, who was pinned to the floor beneath me. From inside me came a voice I didn't recognize—a voice I'd never heard before.

"Don't touch him. Don't ever hit him again."

I didn't need to finish my threat.

Our eyes were locked together in a primal understanding.

My mother had nodded her agreement, and I'd stood, releasing her from beneath my legs. But once she had left my room, I'd fallen back down to the floor, remaining there for a long time afterwards staring at my little brother who was still huddled in the corner crying.

It was the last time that Jeff or I saw that black leather belt. But something changed in me that day. My relationship with my mother, already strained, was broken, and a wall of sorts was erected and sealed off my heart.

It would be a long time before I ever let anyone behind that wall again.

* * *

Twenty-five years, I decided, was long enough to keep a secret. Later that afternoon, over several glasses of wine during lunch, at last I found the courage to tell Peter my truth.

All of it.

"There is something else I need to tell you, Peter," I whispered after I'd finished the first part of the story about my childhood whippings and that fateful day I had pounced on my mother.

He had already absorbed a lot of difficult information for one short lunch, but I knew that if I didn't tell him the whole of it right then and there, I never would.

"What?" he asked in the way people do when they really don't want to know the answer.

I took a deep breath to steady my nerves. And continued.

"Remember how I always told you my mother died in a car..."

CHAPTER 20 - WEDDING RINGS
Alexandria, Virginia, June 1978

I was living in New York for the summer and about to leave for my summer job when the phone rang. Instinctively, I knew that something was amiss. Early morning phone calls have a different sort of ring. They alert our senses, which perhaps, in turn, alter the sound of the ring.

I should have known something was wrong the night before. I had just finished talking on the phone with my father when he said that my mother wanted to speak with me. I was surprised. My mother normally didn't want to speak on the phone with anyone, and certainly not with me. She was very sick at this point, and her Valium dependency had advanced into addiction. As with any addict, her primary, and perhaps only real relationship was with the drug. Our conversation was stilted. We had never had anything significant to say to one another. When I think now about the pain inflicted on me by the repeated beatings, I realize that the suffering I bore was transient. What has endured even to this day is a pain far more devastating than the lash of a leather strap; it's the pain that lies in the fact that I was otherwise ignored by my mother all my life. So I do, and did, know this for sure: My mother had never told me that she loved me. What she had said to me on the phone, then, should have raised my antennae. Except it didn't. My emotions in regard to my mother were completely shut down.

"Hey, I just want you to know one thing, Traci."

"What's that, Mom?"

"That no matter what happens, I love you."

It was the first and only time I had heard her utter those three words to me, and I was so taken aback that I did not know how to respond.

* * *

When the house phone rang, I knew that my life was about to change irrevocably. I felt it on a cellular level. The hair on my arms stood straight up and adrenaline started pumping through my veins. My flight instinct shot to high alert. I wanted to run but couldn't. . . I picked up the phone extension in my bedroom instead. It was my brother.

"Rug is dead."

Rug. My brother had given our mother that nickname because, towards the end of her life, she had taken to having her hair cut short, and it sort of sat on top of her head like a rug.

"Rug is dead," he repeated, as much to make sure that he had said the words clearly as to ensure that I had heard them.

I had indeed heard the words. Our mother was dead, and I could not elicit the simplest response. My mind was racing, and it must have fixed itself on the needs of my brother, dad, and grandmother, because when I finally spoke, all I said was, "I will be on the next plane to DC."

Then I dropped the phone and started screaming.

* * *

Within an hour, Joel and I were sitting on a shuttle headed for Washington, DC. When we emerged in the arrival lounge, I spotted my father and brother, both of them looking disheveled and unshaven. I dropped my small carry-on bag, which hit the tile floor with a sickening thud, and flew into my father's arms. Joel held up my brother, whose knees were buckling under him.

The worst part of our mission still lay ahead of us. We had to tell my grandmother that her beloved firstborn was dead. Thirty minutes later, when the four of us walked into her kitchen, she was drinking her morning coffee and reading the newspaper at the table. I couldn't bear to look at her. I looked at the old yellow stove and refrigerator and at the yellow Formica counters. I studied the pattern of small flowers on the wallpaper. I stared out the window, through its lace curtains. I looked beyond, above, and around but not at her.

She looked at us, each in turn, and she knew that something was very wrong. She stood up and, stumbling backwards, clutched her chest. I thought for a chilling second that we might lose her as well. My father didn't prolong her growing alarm.

"Mary, sit down please."

Ignoring his suggestion and her chair, she continued backing away from us as if she could thereby avoid whatever was coming next. My father followed her stuttered path. He put his arms around her. He spoke softly.

"I am so sorry, but Jean is dead."

She clutched the kitchen counter behind her, steadied herself, and asked an utterly simplistic question.

"How can that be? She is only forty-nine years old."

Again, in consideration of her anxiety, my father did not delay his explanation.

"I'm so sorry, but she killed herself last night, Minnie," my father replied, using my grandmother's sobriquet, given to her due to her shortness.

My grandmother's face twisted into a map of pain. She fell to the ground and, pounding the kitchen floor with her clenched fists, started screaming at the top of her lungs.

"Not my Jean! Not my Jean!"

My father, too, fell to his knees, and with gentle strength, he raised her up. Once she'd regained her composure, she wanted to know how her daughter had died.

My mother had always been a real lady, and she was a lady to the end, even in her suicide. She'd spared us any messy cleanup. No guns, knives or jumps from high windows. Rather, she'd stolen into the closed quarters of the garage after my brother and father had fallen asleep for the night. She'd slipped into the car, started it, and then lain down to wait for the inevitable.

Many years later, I replayed in my head what I imagined to be her last moments, alone in the front seat of our family car in our closed garage. She'd not have felt any pain, of course, nor would she have realized when it was about to happen. She'd have started to drift off, as if she were falling asleep. I wondered if she'd known how close the end lay as she began slipping away. I wondered if, at the last moment, she'd had a change of heart, and in that instant, harbored some flight instinct of her own. But, I think not. My mother had nerves of steel and a determination to match. Once she'd made up her mind to do something she would not be dissuaded by anyone from her mission. She was intent on bringing to an end not only her own suffering but also ours. In her descent, she'd taken us all in varying degrees down with her, and I think that, by her last act, she'd been determined to put a stop to all our suffering. If, then, she'd had any momentary awareness of the first telltale signs of the carbon monoxide's poisoning effect, she would not have had some impulse to run. No, she would have clenched her fists and gritted her teeth. She'd have stayed put and gotten the job done.

She looked peaceful when my father found her, ice-cold, the next morning. He reached into the car's front seat to lift her up without even bothering to try to wake her. He already knew that she was gone. She'd planned her final hours down to the last detail, like her wedding rings, which she'd removed and placed on her nightstand in plain sight, as my father discovered when he woke up. Something was wrong. My mother rarely arose before him, and she never took off her rings.

I can still remember the flowers in the funeral home. As much as I love flowers, the scent of them in their array around a closed casket with my mother's lifeless body inside it, and in a closed room, was overwhelming. I can also remember that I was not at all unhappy when the minister announced it was time to leave for the gravesite. What I cannot remember is a single word that was spoken there. When the service ended, I stood up and took a rose from atop my mother's casket. As I approached the waiting funeral car, I stopped and smelled it. It was beautiful, ivory-white, and despite my reaction to the flowery scents earlier at the funeral parlor, I breathed in its perfume. Then I dropped it in the gutter.

I did not look back as my mother's casket was lowered into the ground. And I never cried a single tear.

Not one.

Not once.

* * *

I was crying now, though, as was the lady at the table next to us. I spared her, as well as Peter, one last unpleasant detail: My mother had committed suicide six weeks before my wedding. I believe it was, in her distorted way of thinking, a wedding present to me—her way to make damn sure she did not mess up my special day.

I also spared myself the full exposure to the secret I had hidden from all my life: the secret that was born over thirty years before, in that quiet, little corner of my childhood bedroom. It would be another five years before I could face it.

PART THREE: ENDINGS AND BEGINNINGS

It matters not how straight the gate,
How charged with punishments the scroll.
I am the master of my fate:
I am the captain of my soul.
—William Ernest Henley

CHAPTER 21 - SETTLEMENT
New York City, June 2008

Pfizer and Ranbaxy began to discuss a possible settlement, and on June 18, we announced the worldwide deal with Ranbaxy.

"The settlement provides shareholders of Pfizer and Ranbaxy, as well as patients, with substantial certainty regarding the potential date—November 30, 2011—for entry of a generic version of Lipitor in the United States. In addition, the agreement provides a license for Ranbaxy to sell generic versions of Lipitor on varying dates in seven additional countries: Canada, Belgium, Netherlands, Germany, Sweden, Italy and Australia. Pfizer and Ranbaxy have also resolved their disputes regarding Lipitor in Malaysia, Brunei, Peru and Vietnam."

Every major newspaper carried the story too. *Bloomberg* honed in on two points: the amount of further Lipitor revenue that the deal secured for Pfizer and the impact of the settlement on Kindler's performance.

"Under a lawsuit settlement, Ranbaxy won't sell generic versions of Lipitor, the world's best-selling drug, until November 2011, New York-based Pfizer said today in a statement. Analysts had projected Ranbaxy would enter the market on March 17, 2010, when the main patent expires. . . Was certainly more joyful—than the St Patrick s Day . . ."

The *Bloomberg* article was succinct as to the impact on Kindler:

"The deal buys Pfizer Chief Executive Officer Jeffrey Kindler more time to find new drugs to replace as much as $12 billion a year at risk when Lipitor copies become available. Investors have been skeptical that Kindler, a former lawyer, can offset the losses with a plan that includes increasing sales of current products, cost cutting and speeding new drugs to market. Since Kindler took command in July 2006, Pfizer, the world's biggest drug maker, has lost 32 percent of its value."

The next day, an article in the *New York Times* made similar points:

"For people with high cholesterol, the wait for a cheaper version of Lipitor has gotten longer. Pfizer has announced an agreement to head off generic competition for its flagship drug until November 2011. The drug maker said Wednesday that it had settled patent litigation with Ranbaxy Laboratories, an Indian maker of generic drugs that had threatened to market its own version of Lipitor, the world's best-selling medicine. The agreement delays Ranbaxy's generic version of Lipitor and is estimated to be worth billions of dollars in additional sales for Pfizer, which could have faced generic competition from Ranbaxy as early as March 2010. Whenever it comes, a cheaper generic version of Lipitor would sharply cut Pfizer's sales of the drug, which were $12.7 billion last year."

* * *

To my astonishment, instead of abounding with events to celebrate a big deal done, my entire world began unraveling soon after the settlement was announced. The following day we received a hold-the-date invite for a celebration party. I was surprised to note that the location was not the customary "to be decided" but rather one of the company's conference rooms instead. I didn't consider it further, figuring that we'd receive an update regarding an actual, high-end restaurant suitable for the occasion.

No update came. On the designated day of celebration, we assembled in the company's conference center for the so-called party. Nonetheless, I tried to rise to the purpose of the occasion. In a heartfelt speech, I thanked everyone who had played a role in achieving the settlement. I simulated the carefree me. I'd become adept at it from the years of practice as a child.

Now, with the settlement behind me, I had no choice but to address what I had been hiding from for the last three months. There was something wrong with both of my arms. I could not lift either above my waist, and it had become all but impossible to get dressed. Nevertheless, it took me another six months to muster the courage to seek medical help.

CHAPTER 22 - DESCENT INTO DARKNESS
New York City, January 2009

Despite my worsening medical condition, 2009 started off on a good note for Pfizer. After two initial rejections, the U.S. Patent Office granted us a notice of allowance in the reissue proceedings of our enantiomer patent. On January 6 Pfizer announced that the company had successfully corrected the technical defect that had resulted in the Court of Appeals loss in 2006.

"Pfizer Inc. announced today that the U.S. Patent & Trademark Office has issued a 'Notice of Allowance' accepting the company's application to correct the technical defect in the '995 enantiomer patent for atorvastatin calcium, the salt form of atorvastatin sold as Lipitor. The company noted that certain formalities must be completed before the reissue patent will be granted. The reissued patent will have the same force and effect as the original '995 patent and the same June 2011 expiration date."

On March 17, our St. Patrick's Day, we had the patent back in our hands, and our day was certainly more joyful than the St. Patrick's Day five years before when I had discovered the first telltale signs of Peter's pancreatic cancer. A company spokesman elaborated on the positive news.

"This is a very positive development, not just for Pfizer but for all those who believe that defending intellectual property is vital to supporting the enormous investments required to develop life-saving new medicines. We have said all along that we had strong arguments for securing the reissue of the patent, and after a vigorous and thorough examination, the Patent Office agreed with this conclusion."

* * *

With the reissue of the Lipitor enantiomer patent secured and the worldwide settlement concluded, I took a vacation for the first time in many years. It was a last, feeble attempt to avoid the inevitable. The Somerset, a lovely resort in Turks & Caicos, and the clear, blue ocean waters offered beauty and serenity, but I could not escape the severity of my emotional and physical problems. Five years of unremitting anxiety and stress had taken their toll. In an island paradise, I was forced to admit what I could no longer evade: I was broken—mind, body and spirit.

On my return to New York, resolved now to address at least the physical problem, I set out to find an orthopedic surgeon. Research led me fast and sure to Dr. Howard in midtown Manhattan. Within minutes of my first visit, he won my confidence. He also confirmed what I had suspected the instant he raised my right arm. To be certain and to ascertain the extent of the damage to the rotator cuff, he scheduled an MRI. The incessant banging and the enclosed space of the scanner were to be the least of the ordeal that I would soon endure.

* * *

At my follow-up appointment, as soon as Dr. Howard walked into the examination room, I knew the news was not good. The look on his face mixed awe with pity.

"There's no easy way to say this, but your rotator cuff tendon is completely severed from the bone."

For a moment, I felt faint and confused. My mind got back its bearings, and I asked the critical question.

"Can you fix it?"

He ignored my question and asked me one instead.

"What pain meds have you been taking?"

"Nothing," I replied with a sigh, and repeated the critical question. "Can you fix it?"

"Yes," he replied. "But there is another issue. Not only is your rotator cuff torn, but the long head of your bicep tendon has slipped out of its groove."

"Can't you just slip it back in when you go in to fix my rotator cuff?" I naïvely asked.

"I'm afraid not," Dr. Howard replied. "Once it's out, it's out."

I paused in my cross-examination to digest it all.

"So what do you want to do?" I asked.

"Well, it's more about what you want to do," he replied.

"You have two options. And this is where you have to make a hard decision."

He paused, took a slight breath, and then pressed on.

"The first is to cut the bicep tendon, which will then roll down the arm and form a pop-eye about here," he said, pointing to the spot on my upper arm where the bulge would appear.

"Or," he continued, "I reattach it to the bone in your arm right about here." Again he pointed to the spot.

"What are the pros and cons of each choice?" I asked.

"Well, if I cut it, there is no pain, no recovery time and no physical therapy after the surgery."

"Sounds good to me," I jumped in before he'd issued his caveat.

"But..." he patiently continued in full disclosure. "You will have a noticeable and unsightly bump in your upper arm, and your bicep muscle will always be weak."

"And if you reattach it?" I moaned.

Instinct was telling me the news was not going to be good, and bravado was not allaying the assault on my nerves.

"Well, no bump, and your arm will be stronger, but the recovery time is long and the post-op pain level can be greater."

My mind went blank. I'm sure my face did too. I had already heard that rotator cuff tears were among the most painful of all sports injuries.

"I know it's a lot to take in," Dr. Howard added with genuine concern. "I'll give you some time to think about it."

In a nanosecond, I said, "Just cut it."

"Are you sure?"

"Yes," I said, pulling the sleeve of my shirt back down.

I thanked him and bolted out of the examining room.

"Make an appointment with my assistant for the surgery when you're ready," Dr. Howard yelled after me as I was fleeing. "And be prepared to miss at least two weeks of work afterwards."

Two weeks of work. What a joke. I hadn't missed two weeks of work in the last twenty years.

* * *

I went back to work and barged into Peter's office.

"Shit!" I screamed. "Shit, shit, shit."

He looked at me over the top of his reading glasses. "I guess you got bad news from the doctor, huh?"

"Worse than bad."

I collected myself enough to recount Dr. Howard's readings of the MRI scan and the options he'd laid out for me in regard to my bicep tendon.

"Don't cut it," Peter said without waiting for me to recite the pros and cons. "You're never going to be happy with half the use of that arm of yours—swimming is way too important to you."

Why argue the point? As usual, Peter was right.

I'd started swimming when I was two years old, and by the time I was six, I was swimming competitively. Swimming had given me my first taste of success, success that I'd shared with my team. It had given me courage, too, and instilled in me the will to win even when I was behind. I remembered the relay race when I was twelve years old: how I had false started, how I'd returned to touch the wall so that my team would not be disqualified—how determined I was, despite the odds, to win. I remembered all the trophies and medals I'd displayed in my childhood room. They'd remind me I was worth something whenever my mother's black leather belt alleged I wasn't.

Peter was right, as usual. I had to attempt a full recovery.

* * *

The surgery—my first ever—was scheduled for Thursday, January 29 at the ambulatory center of Beth Israel Hospital. I don't like hospitals; in fact, I can't think of a place I dislike more. So I'd have done well-nigh anything to avoid walking into that hospital, let alone striding into an operating room and lying down on a cold gurney.

A nurse, solicitous in her well-rehearsed explanation, informed me of the effects of anesthesia, including the warning that, in a very small percentage of cases, the patients may have an allergic reaction and not wake up. Russian roulette with very low odds of the bullet hitting you, but if it does it's lights out, I translated, and interrupted.

"I've got it," I said. "Where do I sign?"

Too soon, I was being led through a set of double doors that separated the patients from their anxious spouses, siblings, relatives, or friends. I looked over my shoulder at Joel, smiled, and mustered a brave little "See you soon." I pressed on so he didn't see my tears.

I entered another waiting area. I felt very much alone, despite the presence of other, no less apprehensive, patients. The atmosphere bred nervousness as all of us, in our blue hospital gowns and slippers, waited for our turns.

Uniformed anxiety.

I noticed among us a young, athletic-looking man. He appeared to be in even worse emotional shape than I was. I left my chair and took the seat next to him.

"Hey, what wonderful thing is happening to you today?" I asked as jovially as I could.

"Rotator cuff repair."

I gave him a sympathetic nod.

"Me too. How did you tear yours?"

"I'm a baseball pitcher."

I felt sick to my stomach. At my last appointment with Dr. Howard, he'd mentioned baseball players as another group of athletes who suffered from rotator cuff tears, along with tennis players and swimmers, but with a bleaker prognosis.

I tried to imagine how this young baseball pitcher must feel at the prospect of his career disappearing like a sinker. I tried to be upbeat.

"Everyone says that if you do physical therapy two to three times a week for a year, you're as good as new. Right?"

He gave me a hopeful look, and tears started streaming down my face. I hoped he'd think he was witnessing the effect of my pre-surgery nerves and not the shame I felt at offering him hollow assurances. I felt awful for him.

Suddenly I heard a voice from across the room.

"Medford."

If it was like being called from the dugout, speaking of baseball, it also summoned me back to the moment. I raised my hand, admitting to being the "guilty" party and then jumped up and started to follow the nurse to the operating room. And stopped. I glanced over my shoulder at the young pitcher, his head bowed. Seized by an impulse I still can't explain, I ran back across the waiting room floor, slipping and sliding in those stupid little hospital slippers they make you wear, and gave the sad, young pitcher a big kiss on the cheek.

He gave me a dazzling smile in return. It set my heart at ease for a brief moment.

The operating room was freezing. I was lying on a gurney. My left arm was outstretched and tied down as if for an execution. At my side, the anesthesiologist was inserting the IV that would transport me to Neverland, where my shoulder would be made "young" again. In reality, though, I lay alone and vulnerable in a cold, stark, sterile room without the comfort or support of a friend. Policy required it; asepsis above all . . . and then . . .

I was in the recovery room. Joel was smiling down at me. There is no sense of the passage of time during a surgery performed under general anesthesia, but there is a great sense of relief when you wake up.

I cried again.

I had survived.

* * *

One week after surgery I returned to the office with my arm in a sling. The inability to use my writing hand, coupled with a high level of post-op pain, made working difficult. I had three weeks to get myself back together before physical therapy began.

Time alone cannot heal an injury to a rotator cuff nor repair one. Unlike the recovery from most surgical wounds, rotator cuff repair requires dedication to extensive post-op physical therapy before the arm regains its full range of motion and, thereafter, its strength. Two to three days each week. Week in, week out. The therapy is difficult—you expect that—but it's also excruciatingly painful.

I felt like I'd fallen down a deep hole, and not into any Wonderland, that allowed me no choice but by hand and knee to crawl out. So crawl I did, even though I had to do it without pain meds in order to think halfway clearly. I threw out the meds and endured a post-op pain level that exceeded anything I had ever experienced. At the same time, I battled with denial. I could not confess to myself—let alone Dr. Howard during my follow-up visit—that my left rotator cuff was shot as well. With unbearable post-surgery pain in my right arm and the intense pain generated by the unrepaired tear in my left, I chose instead to bury my head in the sand.

I was not, however, on the beach in Turks & Caicos.

CHAPTER 23 - HERE WE GO AGAIN
New York City, January–May 2009

A few days before my surgery, Pfizer had announced its third major merger in less than a decade. Again, it was a household name: Wyeth. The news had not been met with a completely favorable public reception. An example was Jim Edwards' January article in his Money Watch column:

"Today's announcement that Pfizer is to acquire Wyeth for $68 billion eclipsed some things that on any other day would have been headline news in themselves: a) The fact that Pfizer's earnings were down 90 percent due to a $2.3 billion settlement with the Department of Justice over its off-label promotion of Bextra, the Cox-2 painkiller, and b) the new company plans 19,000 layoffs to make its deal work."

Edwards was equally concerned about the proposed dividend cut to pay for the merger:

"That's not the only questionable event lurking behind the $68 billion dollar topline. We also learn that Pfizer is to halve its dividend payments to 16 cents a share to help pay for the acquisition. Unsurprisingly, PFE shares dropped this morning. Wyeth holders may be getting a payday, but Pfizer holders are taking a bath."

To back up his criticism, Edwards quoted Kindler's comment about the previous two mega-mergers with Warner-Lambert and Pharmacia:

"Those acquisitions definitely hurt morale and hurt productivity, no doubt about it."

Spring-boarding off *Bloomberg's* summation of the acquisition, Edwards offered an even more unflattering one of his own:

"So morale will certainly plummet at Wyeth, where they've seen the 16,000 jobs lost at Pfizer; and Pfizer, where employees could have been forgiven for thinking they were nearing the end of the job cuts. Turning a $70 billion behemoth composed of two giant, different, corporate cultures into a single, nimble, unified force will be a 'challenge,' as they say in management-land."

While analysts may vary in their estimations of the effect that mergers have on corporations and the employees, most of them agree on the soundness of one simple mathematical formula: Turmoil increases fear, which, in turn, reduces productivity. Catherine Arnst's article in *Bloomberg* on January 26 captured some of the more difficult challenges facing Pfizer:

"Kindler told a news conference that the Wyeth merger is not about a 'single product or cost cutting,' as with past deals. Instead, 'it's about creating a broad, diversified portfolio.' Nevertheless, cost cutting there will be. Pfizer expects to achieve about $4 billion in 'synergies' by 2012, enabling it to reduce the combined workforce of the two companies by 15% or some 20,000 jobs. As part of those synergies, Pfizer announced on Monday that it will eliminate 8,000 jobs, 10% of its workforce."

Despite the merger announcement, the Pfizer stock price continued its decline. On March 2 it hit its all-time low at $11.66 a share. When Kindler had taken over as CEO on July 28, 2006 it had closed at $26.11. Only six years earlier, it had traded as high as $49.25.

* * *

With Peter's retirement date set for November, I was now the acting head of the group, and in the current transition period, Peter was serving as my advisor. The situation was awkward, to say the least, since, for the past twenty years, I had been reporting to him.

I had just learned the names of the additional, new Pfizer colleagues who'd be reporting to me, and now, with another merger a sure thing, I'd be responsible for integrating all the Wyeth colleagues—or, rather, those who'd keep their jobs.

Before we could address the personnel issues, however, we had to review the Wyeth patent portfolio—no easy task, especially as I'd be on the injured list for quite a while. With mandatory, three-hour physical therapy appointments three days a week, I was losing nine hours of office time each week. I had to make up that lost time by working late and on the weekends.

The eventual merger with Wyeth brought over one hundred intellectual property colleagues to our group, each of whom had to be interviewed with great care because not all of them could be retained in the new combined organization. Our Wyeth colleagues were, of course, aware that a number of their jobs were at risk, and that awareness intensified their anxiety and fear.

Under normal circumstances, I didn't worry when a patent lawyer lost a job. In patent law, the ratio of available jobs to an eligible patent attorney was about ten to one. In 2009, however, circumstances were not normal. The economy was going from bad to worse. Unemployment rates were rising. House prices were dropping. The mortgage crisis was in full swing. The only upside for the pharmaceutical industry was that the bad-boy reputation we'd inherited from the tobacco industry had now been passed on to the bankers and Wall Street.

* * *

Despite the stunning success of the Lipitor settlement, there were still a dozen or so other Lipitor cases pending trial.

It was also a tough time for me personally. My right arm was in a sling, and Peter had announced his retirement. Moreover, my team members had worked themselves into the ground, their personal relationships having suffered as a result. I felt responsible.

I was still unable to swim, and although I didn't know it then, it would be another two years before I could. So, in an effort to stave off my rapid weight gain, I had started working out on the treadmill. The routine may have trimmed my waistline, but it did nothing for my foot. I developed a whopping case of Morton's neuroma, a thickening of the tissue around the nerve that travels between the third and fourth toes. I was barely able to limp through the halls, much less make the daily commute to work. For all my attempts to ignore or minimalize the condition, by April, it was clear that I was going to need more surgery, my second in less than three months. I put on a brave face and quipped to my staff.

"I'm getting to know every ambulatory operating room in New York City."

Two days after the foot surgery, I hobbled back into the office. With a cast on my foot and my arm still in a sling, I looked a sight.

"Here comes the walking wounded, no pun intended," Peter said jokingly, trying to make light of a situation that was going from bad to worse.

"Oh, ha-bloody-ha, as you would say, Peter."

I laughed too. Only there wasn't much time for it. We had work to do.

"Are we ever going to get a break and get back to normal?" Will frequently asked, although he already knew the answer.

Normal had become a memory in a world in which we were working sixty-plus hours a week.

"Working this hard is the reason I left the law firm," Charlotte informed me.

I felt helpless.

"And besides, I'd like to have a baby before it's too late," Charlotte added. "But I can't even find the time to have a date night with my husband," she noted.

"I know, Charlotte," I said, unable to gloss over the reality.

Will was listening carefully and nodding. "Let's face it," he interjected. "It's not just us. Everyone's spouse or significant other dislikes Corporate America at this point."

My own husband's face flashed before my eyes.

Oh boy.

CHAPTER 24 – AU REVOIR
New York City, November 2009

Despite the waves of corporate layoffs, the most difficult exit for me personally was Peter's imminent retirement. Too soon, we were nearing the day we would be bidding him goodbye. His thirty-three years of service warranted a party, but all the recent belt-tightening didn't allow us money for a lavish one. We decided instead upon a small affair at a nearby French restaurant. For me, the evening was bound to be bittersweet; only it was more so than expected. A French restaurant summoned from my memory all the times Peter and I had traveled to Paris, for one or another of our business meetings, and in my mind, I could travel back in time to an era when both Pfizer and I were healthy and happy. It helped to ward off the emptiness rising from the pit of my stomach. I had worked with Peter for a quarter of a century. We had traveled the world together; worldwide, we'd fought off challenges to Pfizer's patents together. Together was now over.

The day I dreaded, even feared, arrived—November 30, 2009. I couldn't help but be struck at the coincidence of the November 30 date. It brought to an end the career of a giant among litigators; two years later, it would mark the end of a giant among pharmaceuticals—Lipitor as we knew it. How could I have known at the time that yet a third November 30 date would soon herald grave consequences as well?

I did not want to see Peter retire. Indeed, I had been begging, borrowing, and stealing more time from him for years. He was almost sixty-eight years old; enough was enough. We were having lunch one day at a favorite hangout on Lexington Avenue, and I was at it again.

"Can't you just stay until next spring?" I pleaded.

Peter looked up from his plate, in his over-the-top-of-his-reading-glasses way.

"Come on, Traci. Even a train stops."

At that same moment, the song "Time to Say Goodbye" began to play on the restaurant's piped-in music channel, and I heard my father's voice in my head. Only this time, it did not tell me not to be afraid.

This time, it said, "Traci, let go."

Reluctantly, I did.

But I struggled emotionally, even more than usual, for the next several months. Except for the period of Peter's illness in 2004, I had spent the last twenty-five years of my professional life working with him hand in glove. He had become my only anchor in uncertain, turbulent waters. Without him, I was lost in a storm that would soon rage out of control and leave me swimming, alone and very afraid, in a shark-infested sea.

CHAPTER 25 - MANY MASTERS
New York, January–June 2010

As 2009 passed into 2010, Pfizer was busy adjusting to its latest acquisition. And it seemed, marching to the beat of many drums. A primary focus was on our third big merger in less than a decade.

"Pfizer's newly strengthened company will have some of the best assets, people, pipeline and capabilities in the industry," Kindler asserted in the press announcement.

The news was hitting every major newspaper at the time, with some of the less supportive commentary focusing on the number of jobs that would be eliminated and other cost-cutting measures that had been implemented. Jim Edwards's article in *Money Watch* was but one example.

"To give you an idea of the cost-cutting misery going on at Pfizer right now, take a look at Café Pharma, the anonymous gossip site for pharmaceutical industry workers. One thread, titled 'Being forced to room with someone at meetings is so degrading and dehumanizing,' has had more than 10,000 views from Pfizer employees (and those interested in them), thousands more than any of the other Pfizer threads. It describes Pfizer's morale-killing policy of requiring drug sales reps and other executives to double up in hotel rooms when they are on the road to save money."

Edwards continued his *Money Watch* article with a follow-up as to how the executives were faring under the new belt-tightening regime, which I felt was particularly unfair.

"Meanwhile, Pfizer's top executives are flying around the world in three private planes and six helicopters. So the news that Pfizer will lay off more than the 19,000 staff it estimated when it merged with Wyeth in 2009 to form a 129,500-employee colossus will come with a special sting."

I knew all of Pfizer's "top executives," and they were not taking advantage of our planes or helicopters. However to back up his critique, Edwards quoted from the Pfizer SEC report itself:

"At the end of the third quarter of 2010, the workforce totaled approximately 111,500, a decrease of 5,000 from December 31, 2009. Since the closing of the Wyeth acquisition on October 15, 2009, the workforce has declined by 9,200, primarily in the U.S. Primary Care field force, manufacturing, R & D and corporate operations. We expect to exceed our original 15% workforce reduction target."

As I read Edwards' articles, I thought about my colleagues who no longer worked at Pfizer, and I wondered who else would be included in the latest reduction target.

Would it be someone on my team?

Would it be me?

That Edwards was not happy with Pfizer's current operations was clear enough, but none of us knew exactly what path the company should follow at this juncture. For sure, I didn't have all the answers; I felt, in fact, that I'd never had fewer. What I did know was that Pfizer was trying to do its best, but the external environment had become a formidable opponent for all of Big Pharma. In addition to the one-sided scheme under which each and every patent could be challenged, the imminent expiration of the patents on numerous blockbuster drugs, the continued research difficulties and shrinking pipelines, it was also becoming more difficult to obtain FDA approval for the new drugs that were discovered. Except for generics. On top of all of this, the industry was not held in high esteem by the general public. Nevertheless, Wall Street expected everyone to make their numbers, and then we were criticized for trying to reduce costs in order to do so.

At times, it felt that nothing we did was right.

* * *

Opinions on Pfizer's latest merger and cost-cutting measures were soon eclipsed, however, by the ongoing media coverage of the raging debate over the impending Congressional vote on Obamacare. Not only were Republicans and Democrats sharply divided, it seemed as though the entire country was.

Everyone had something to say about Big Pharma's role in it. Early rumors about secret deals made with the White House were becoming front page news. An internal memo dated July 7, 2009 outlining the suspected secret deal had been discovered, and the press had picked up the story. On September 9 the Huffington Post headline had confirmed its existence:

"Internal Memo Confirms Big Giveaways in White House Deal with Big Pharma."

The story had elaborated on the finding.

"A memo obtained by the Huffington Post confirms that the White House and the pharmaceutical lobby secretly agreed to precisely the sort of wide-ranging deal that both parties have been denying over the past week.

It says the White House agreed to oppose any congressional efforts to use the government's leverage to bargain for lower drug prices or import drugs from Canada—and also agreed not to pursue Medicare rebates or shift some drugs from Medicare Part D, which would cost Big Pharma billions in reduced reimbursements.

In exchange the Pharmaceutical Researchers and Manufacturers Association (PhRMA) agreed to cut $80 billion in projected costs to taxpayers and senior citizens over ten years."

Despite its existence, both PhRMA and the White House had adamantly denied that the July 7 memo reflected reality. PhRMA senior vice president, Ken Johnson, said that the July 7 outline "is simply not accurate."

* * *

On March 23, 2010, with the exact nature of the so-called secret deal still in question, but the rumors and criticism of the industry abounding, history was made when Obamacare was passed. The *New York Times* was among the literally thousands of newspapers to carry the story.

"With the strokes of 22 pens, President Obama signed his landmark health care overhaul—the most expansive social legislation enacted in decades—into law on Tuesday, saying it enshrines 'the core principle that everybody should have some basic security when it comes to their health care.'

Mr. Obama signed the measure, the Patient Protection and Affordable Care Act, during a festive and at times raucous ceremony in the East Room of the White House. He spoke to an audience of nearly 300, including more than 200 Democratic lawmakers who rode a yearlong legislative roller coaster that ended with House passage of the bill Sunday night. They interrupted him repeatedly with cheers, applause and standing ovations."

* * *

In May, with the frenzy over Obamacare quieting down and the Wyeth merger old news, the media focus shifted yet again. Rumors about Pfizer's attempt to do a high-level deal with the German generic company, Ratiopharm, were confirmed when Kindler was spotted in Ulm, Germany meeting with Ratiopharm's top executives. The sighting prompted a joke: "There's no place like Ulm." Not so jokingly, we learned that Pfizer was engaged in a public bidding war with the Israel-based Teva Pharmaceutical Industries over the German generic biologic company. In the end, Teva won out.

On May 18, The *Wall Street Journal* headlined the battle in a terse eight words:

"Teva Outwrestles Pfizer to Land Generics Maker Ratiopharm."

The article went on to explain, in part what might have motivated Pfizer to pursue the deal in the first place.

"Pfizer, facing the expiration of patent protection on Lipitor starting next year, the biggest selling drug of all time, has been shifting away from the blockbuster drug model and embracing more diversification through avenues such as generics."

I had to agree, if reluctantly, that diversification might not be a bad idea, given the environment in which all of Big Pharma now had to operate. Nevertheless, a move like that would have amounted to a veritable seismic shift for a company that had been on the research end of the business for over a hundred years. It was also a seismic shift for me, having spent the last twenty-five years battling against generics.

* * *

As perplexed as I was about Big Pharma's role in the passage of Obamacare, as well as with the latest turn of events in the office, I had more pressing personal issues that I needed to resolve. I had already paid a huge physical price for years of intense, job-related stress, and much of the joy I'd experienced in the office had departed with Peter. Stress, of course, came with the job, and my added responsibilities at the helm were not diminishing it.

For months, my husband had been encouraging me to retire before my health got even worse. Then, one night as we were walking home from dinner, he stopped right in the middle of Park Avenue, threw his hands up in the air and shouted at the top of his lungs.

"Save yourself! Save yourself! Please, Traci, do something before you get cancer and die!"

He was right. I had to do something. Not only was the stress of work starting to affect my health, which had always been good up until that point, but I was also suffering from the physical pain in my left shoulder that I could no longer ignore. I felt like a prisoner trapped in my own body.

I wasn't quite ready to retire, but I did visit Dr. Howard's office again in June.

* * *

Another MRI. Another follow-up visit. Again, the look mixing awe with pity was on Dr. Howard's face when he entered the same small examination room, and I was not surprised when he again delivered the same news.

"I'm so sorry, Traci. You were right. Your left rotator cuff is torn, too, and it is not healing. But at least your bicep tendon is intact."

I had only one question.

"Let me ask you something, Dr. Howard. How many of your patients have had two rotator cuff repair surgeries?"

I knew by now that Dr. Howard was "Mr. Rotator Cuff Repair" in New York City. He performed, on average, four repairs a week, as he had been doing for over twenty years. That's a lot of surgeries and a lot of patients, so I was astonished by his answer.

"None."

Again, the look, only this time, the pity overshadowed the awe. For the first time in my life, I felt sorry for myself too.

* * *

The routine at the hospital, though now more familiar, was no less terrifying. I was grateful that I did not have to sit through a reprise of the statistics vis-à-vis patients who experience allergic reactions to anesthesia. When the doctor inserted the IV into my arm, I was pretty sure I'd not be counted among the unlucky few who never wake up—not that pretty certain is entirely comforting when you're talking about your life. So, in those last few precious moments of consciousness, I did what many of us do when our backs are up against the wall—or, in this case, down against the cold slab of an operating table.

I prayed.

When, on my return home later that day, the numbness in my left arm receded, I was taken aback by the unanticipated intensity of pain. I'd survived a similar level of it the year before, yet I'd not retained the memory of it. The mind can be a powerful amnesiac. I realized at the same moment that another year of dedicated physical therapy appointments would dominate my calendar. I felt diminished, weak, and defeated even before the battle had begun. I realized, too, with absolute certainty that I had reached my own personal inflection point.

So I did something that I had only ever done once before.

I fell to my knees and begged.

For help.

For forgiveness.

For mercy.

CHAPTER 26 - HARD CHOICES
New York City, July–December 2010

The summer and fall of 2010 brought a series of difficult transitions.

Recovery from the second rotator cuff repair was proving to be much more arduous than the first. My husband continued to implore me to do something before it was too late. Less than a year ago, I'd begged Peter to stay, but I now had to concede that he'd been right to retire. After all, every train does have to stop at some point. My last official day at the company was August 30, 2010. Kindler's own departure would follow just three months later.

The end of a career. It had been a long one. Thirty years. For the most part, too, it had been a fulfilling and pleasant one. I'd not ever given much thought to the idea of retirement; so the sudden and unexpected fact of it required more than a minute for me to get my bearings, not to mention setting my team, in my absence, on a feasible course.

My decline was mental as well as physical. I'd had three surgeries in less than sixteen months. I'd become reliant on medicine to control my daily migraines, and my lower back, never strong to begin with, was now in a constant state of spasms. I was having anxiety attacks, but I simply couldn't face another doctor's appointment to determine with certainty their nature and cause. And Joel was at his wit's end. Having already paid a high physical and emotional price for my involvement with the Lipitor case, I was not prepared to sacrifice what was left of my strained marriage as well.

Without question, I knew I needed to move on. That knowledge, however, did not make my last day at the office or the ensuing transition to retirement any easier. Or the isolation of it. I felt the way I had after a long swim race—standing but not yet quite stable. For the first time in three decades, I was on the outside looking in—a nobody in my professional life. I still hadn't figured it out that I was always a nobody. I was still under the illusion that I had once been a somebody. I knew I was not alone in these feelings. Many of my friends and family members, as well as thousands of American workers, suddenly found themselves unemployed during this time period.

I quickly lost track of most of my professional colleagues who were once among my best friends. That was very difficult for me. People who would have quickly answered my emails when I was still Chief IP Counsel were now ignoring me. I no longer had any chits to trade. So not only was I fighting to regain my health, I was also searching for a way to reinvent myself in the hope of being a somebody again. It was one of the more difficult periods of my life, and more than once, despite not belonging to a church, I found myself inside a house of worship, on my knees, or both.

* * *

Sunday night, December 5, 2010.

My ear-to-the-ground brother was on the phone, and again I was shocked by the news he was delivering.

"Your man Kindler . . ."

He began the conversation the same way he had four years earlier when he'd called to tell me that Kindler had been named CEO.

"Not exactly my man," I said. "But what's up?"

"He's out."

"Of favor?"

"Of Pfizer!"

"Holy shit!"

"Holy shit is right, Traci."

The board had named Ian Read as the new CEO. That night, Pfizer's press release announcing Kindler's resignation offered a partial explanation for his abrupt departure in a quote by Kindler himself:

"The combination of meeting the requirements of our many shareholders around the world and the 24/7 nature of my responsibilities has made this period extremely demanding on me personally."

Earlier that day, Kindler and Pfizer had agreed on an exit package: $16 million in cash and stock, $6.9 million in retirement benefits, and various other forms of stock compensation as well.

As I read the press announcement, I remembered our outstanding and sweeping Lipitor victory in 2005 and all the notes of congratulations.

But we were both gone now. Did it matter any longer?

* * *

Eventually, though not without considerable difficulty, I found a new beginning—two, in fact.

First, I opened a Nuevo Latino restaurant, Ramiro's 954, in upstate New York. My husband did not react favorably when I announced the news.

"Are you crazy, Traci? What do you know about the restaurant business?"

"Not a single thing," I answered honestly.

"You're going to need some help," he replied with a worried look on his face.

"Great, you can be one of my partners then," I exclaimed with delight.

Second, I set up a law firm with Peter—Richardson & Rosow—which was conveniently located in midtown Manhattan near our old hangouts. Peter was likewise a bit reluctant when I announced this plan.

"Traci, come on, we're retired now. It's time to put ourselves out to pasture and let the young bucks take over."

"Come on," I pleaded. "I can't explain why, but I just have my gut feeling," I said trying to jostle him into agreement

Reluctantly, he did.

Through it all, I attended my second year-long round of PT appointments. The fall passed busily and painfully. I spent a lot of time praying for my recovery.

And for the strength to endure it.

CHAPTER 27 - DIRTY LAUNDRY
New York City, March–September 2011

Spring came early in 2011, and the restaurant and law firm started to blossom along with the hyacinths and tulips. The law firm got its first few clients, and the restaurant was steadily gaining customers. I was regaining both my mental and physical bearings.

On June 10 the restaurant received the highest rating possible from the *New York Times*. The review gave us a serious boost in popularity. The incognito critic loved everything, but she highlighted in particular my partner's brilliant use of flavors and textures to create a unique dining experience.

"Only four months old, this restaurant is already lively with sophisticated diners who tend to pass on Tex-Mex salsa, chips and refried beans. Mr. Jimenez balances textures and flavor subtly and brilliantly; his seasonings lead diners through a sequence of tastes that surprise and delight."

The praise, as with many things in life, had its negative side too. We were suddenly packed and unable to handle the demand. This resulted in stepping on our own feet more than once.

But fortune struck a second time, thus forgiving us some of our foot-stepping sins, on September 2 when the restaurant was featured on the ABC *Eyewitness News* in the weekly "Neighborhood Eats" segment hosted by Lauren Glassberg.

Watching the ABC news on the big screen TV in the restaurant was a surreal experience for all of us.

Less auspiciously, however, earlier in the year, I had received a phone call from a *Fortune* magazine reporter who wanted to interview me about what had gone on inside Pfizer's corporate headquarters during the time of Kindler's tenure. I knew at once that trouble was brewing again. I refused to talk with him.

Many of my other colleagues apparently did not feel likewise constrained.

* * *

July 28, 2011.

The phone rang. Peter.

"Hey, have you seen the *Fortune* article?"

"Yes, just finished reading it."

"Can you believe the timing of it?" I asked.

"What do you mean?"

"It is dated July 28. Five years to the day since Kindler was named CEO."

Timing aside, the article, entitled "Inside Pfizer's Palace Coup," by Peter Elkind and Jennifer Reingold, was an account of the last four years at Pfizer.

Although I'd known that the Fortune article was in the works since the reporter had contacted me that spring, I was not prepared for the shock of it in print. There it was in black and white, but filled with graphic, gaudy, and colorful details: the policy wars, the personality clashes, and the power plays. The portrait it drew of Kindler himself emerged in the abundance of quotations from Pfizer associates, none of them flattering.

Bill Steere, Pfizer's former CEO and once one of Kindler's staunchest supporters, related an unfortunate occasion on which Kindler had lost control of his temper in front of a board member. Steere had reportedly taken Kindler aside and reminded him, "Screaming at board members is not a good business plan."

The article recounted, too, the unusual December meeting between three board members and Kindler, who'd been summoned at only twenty-four hours' notice. The board members, according to the article, "...confronted Kindler with questions about his management and his behavior. Had he routinely berated subordinates? Did he really bring senior executives to tears? And how did he respond to charges that his leadership style, a sort of micro-micro-management, had paralyzed Pfizer?"

The article elaborated on Kindler's behavior:

"Kindler's tendency to grill people in public made other team members cringe. Kindler could be remorseful after letting loose—he'd send women flowers the day after bringing them to tears—but that didn't prevent the next explosion."

I felt a strange array of emotions. But, for the most part, I just felt sad. I also felt it was unfair to blame Kindler, or anyone, for what had happened at Pfizer. The problems Pfizer faced were systemic in nature and shared by all of Big Pharma. The constant attacks on its intellectual property, the ever-increasing difficulties in finding new drugs despite the billions of dollars spent on research, the reluctance by the FDA to grant health approvals, all of which had necessitated extreme cost-reduction measures and layoffs, had finally taken its toll on the entire industry.

Peter and I discussed the *Fortune* article for the next hour. Neither of us could quite figure out how the reporters had managed to get all their information.

"Someone at a very high level must have fed them quite a bit of inside scoop," Peter said.

"The whole thing is so sad and unfair," I replied with a sigh.

"Hmmm," Peter mumbled solemnly.

Elkind and Reingold were less subtle in their portrayal of the changes in Pfizer:

"Once a corporate icon and Wall Street darling, Pfizer has tumbled into disarray. In the decade that ended with Kindler's departure, its stock price sagged from a high of $49 down to $17 and its drug pipeline dried up (problems the company continues to grapple with today). Pfizer lost its way, stumbling through a frantic series of zigzags in the hopes of finding new blockbusters to sustain its prodigious profits in the future."

CHAPTER 28 - END OF AN ERA
New York City, November 2011

Despite my struggles, in the months following the publication of the article in *Fortune* magazine, I found more to be grateful for than not. The restaurant was named one of the best new eateries of 2011, thus giving it its third booster shot that year.

Carol had graduated from Hofstra Law School. Peter and I had attended her graduation. The thrill that we had felt when she had walked across the stage to receive her diploma was unequalled by any litigation victory we had achieved in our thirty years of working together.

Peter remained cancer free.

Charlotte had had her first child, a daughter. Will, our Mr. Peter Pan, had become a first-time father to a son.

The law firm continued to flourish, as well as an educational charity that Peter and I ran in our limited spare time, the College Educational Milestone Foundation. The foundation, which I had created in 2009 in memory of my father, was dedicated to providing funds for high performing college students who lacked the financial means to pay for tuition. Despite our limited resources, we had managed to support quite a few deserving young students.

I had regained the strength in both my arms, and at last, I was swimming again. And so, I thought I had finally broken free of the past—that my own personal inflection point had finally reached the upward point on the curve. But then, what we had all known could happen, did happen—plaintiff lawsuits, they're called by antitrust lawyers. They grow like mushrooms in the dark, and they are of the dangerous variety.

Under the terms of our settlement agreement, Ranbaxy could begin selling its generic copy of Lipitor on November 30, 2011. The press was all over it. The sick needed cheaper medicine; the rich pharmaceutical company was at last getting its just deserts. It was a big story heralding a much-awaited event—for the nine million American patients taking Lipitor, for the pharmacists who sold it, and for the insurers who paid for it.

So I guess I should not have been that surprised when, on the morning of November 8, a news story reported that the first antitrust lawsuit had been filed in California. Ten more soon followed, but they only foretold the tidal wave of suits that would swamp Pfizer by the spring. The Chimes Pharmacies vs. Pfizer lawsuit alleged that Pfizer and Ranbaxy, as well as both companies' previous CEOs, had entered into a conspiracy and an illegal settlement. The plaintiffs demanded disgorgement of profits, trebled, thus making the soon-to-be consolidated lawsuit one of the largest antitrust cases in the U.S.

When my morning eyes cleared, I read the *Bloomberg* story a second time.

"Pfizer Inc. and Ranbaxy Laboratories Ltd. were accused by 11 California pharmacies in a lawsuit of agreeing to hold back a generic version of the cholesterol-lowering drug Lipitor in the U.S. and then fixing its price. As a result of an unlawful agreement with generic-maker Ranbaxy, Pfizer was able to make $18 billion by extending its time as the exclusive U.S. source of Lipitor, the pharmacies claimed in a lawsuit filed Nov. 7 in federal court in San Francisco. In exchange, Pfizer allegedly allowed Ranbaxy to distribute the generic of Lipitor earlier in foreign markets. The lawsuit seeks disgorgement of profits from the allegedly illegal arrangement and triple damages."

I put down my iPad and called Peter.

"Can you believe this shit?"

"Traci, I'm still asleep. Can you call me back later?"

Undeterred, I continued my rant.

"Lipitor hasn't even gone off patent yet, and the scavengers are already circling the body."

The key date was still more than three weeks away: November 30, 2011. The news story seemed to interest Peter less than it did me.

"There is nothing we can do about any of this now that we are both retired," Peter stated the obvious.

"I know, but the body is not yet even cold," I sighed.

However, many of the bodies that had played key roles in the Lipitor litigation and settlement were, if not cold, gone from the precincts of Pfizer.

I had spent the better part of the past year rebuilding my family and professional life, my mind, and my body. They were all hard-fought, semi-victories. Top among the very last things I wanted to do in this life, ever again, was to get involved with a Lipitor case. Nevertheless, I wondered how long it would be before I was dragged back into the drama. Of more concern, I wondered whether I could withstand another Lipitor battle. While I was getting better every day, I was very far from being healed. I knew I'd have some more time to get stronger before the case got going, and I set my mind on doing just that.

CHAPTER 29 – VIVA OBAMACARE!
Washington D.C., June 2012

In June another series of news articles connected Pfizer to the passage of Obamacare. My husband brought the paper in from our driveway and laid it on the kitchen counter.

"Well, you were right," he said. "Here it is in black and white!"

I glanced at the headlines. It stood out prominently on the front page of the June 8 *New York Times*:

"Obama was Pushed by the Drug Industry."

The article spared very few details, including dates when Kindler was at the White House:

"After weeks of talks, drug industry lobbyists were growing nervous. To cut a deal with the White House on overhauling healthcare, they needed to be sure that President Obama would stop a proposal intended to bring down medicine prices."

They—the healthcare lobbyists—got the assurance they needed in emails that had now come to light. The *Times* article quoted from these emails:

"Although Mr. Obama was overseas. . . top officials had 'made a decision, based on how constructive you guys have been, to oppose importation' on a different proposal."

To make sure that readers understood the import of these email exchanges, the *Times* summarized what it considered to be an unhealthy bargain:

"Just like that, Mr. Obama's staff signaled a willingness to put aside support for the reimportation of prescription medicines at lower prices, and by doing so solidified a compact with an industry the president had vilified on the campaign trail. Central to Mr. Obama's drive to remake the nation's healthcare system was an unlikely collaboration with the pharmaceutical industry that forced unappealing trade-offs."

The Times did balance its criticism of Obama's decision with a rationalization for his willingness to cut the deal:

"But the bargain was one that the president deemed necessary to forestall industry opposition that had thwarted efforts to cover the uninsured for generations. Without the deal, in which the industry agreed to provide $80 billion to expand coverage in exchange for protection from policies that would cost more, Mr. Obama calculated he might get nowhere."

The Republicans were not so kind. Congress knew some sort of deal between PhRMA (Pharmaceutical Research and Manufacturers of America) and the administration was in the works, and the Republican Congressional Committee staff kept digging for dirt. With the long-awaited Supreme Court decision on the constitutionality of Obamacare being expected any day, and the November elections only a few months away, the digging was frantic.

The *Wall Street Journal* advanced the story on June 11:

"Obamacare's Secret History, How a Pfizer CEO and Big Pharma Colluded with the White House at the Public's Expense."

Pfizer and Kindler were singled out.

"The business refrain in those days was that if you're not at the table, you're on the menu. But it turns out Big Pharma was also serving as head chef, maître d'hôtel and dishwasher. Though some parts of the story have been reported before, the emails make clear that Obamacare might never have passed without the drug companies. Thank you, Pfizer."

I felt the criticism of both sides to be unfair and shortsighted. Obamacare had secured healthcare coverage for millions of uninsured Americans. The pharmaceutical companies had made a significant contribution to that success. In the process, they had been thrown a crumb from a feast otherwise enjoyed by nonparticipants in the battle. Yet both sides were tarred and feathered.

Whatever the specifics, the deal itself was undisputable at this point. All eyes were now on the Supreme Court and the long-awaited decision that was the result of whatever agreement the industry had cut with the administration. It seemed that just about everyone's lives had been affected by the healthcare debate. But the people who would be the most affected by the imminent Supreme Court decision were those who needed the law to be upheld the most—the people with pre-existing conditions who could not get health insurance at any price.

As the country waited for the decision to come down, the political machines were working overtime producing fodder. I closed my laptop. My eyes were tired. Thursday June 21, the longest day in the calendar year, the official start of summer, had come and gone without the Supreme Court decision. It would be Monday now, at the earliest, before the decision would issue.

I was used to waiting for court decisions. More than twenty-five years of patent litigation had made it so. But the media weren't as patient. For days, they had reported every rumor. Every prediction. Every opinion. There were even press stories about the press stories.

How would the Supreme Court write the ending?

The world was waiting.

For Democrats it meant the possible overturning of what they had fought so long and hard to achieve. Even if the idea of extending health care coverage to more Americans had originally been a Republican led initiative. But that had long since been forgotten. Now it was about political maneuvering and using the Supreme Court decision as political fodder for the presidential election that was less than five months away.

As the days passed without a decision, more people jumped on the "unconstitutional" bandwagon, and the tension continued to mount. Congressional members had returned to Washington over the weekend in preparation. Staff were standing ready. Press conferences had been pre-arranged. Even space on the Capital Hill lawns had been staked out for post-decision interviews. Despite Congressional members having some of the best health care insurance of anyone in this country, they all had something to say about the men, women and children who had none.

Just minutes into the Monday court session, a decision was issued. Car radios were turned up. People stopped jumping from one TV channel to another. Live blogs would report the news as fast as it came in. The Supreme Court had ruled on a long-awaited decision. But it wasn't on Obamacare. They ruled on the Arizona immigration issue instead. Very important to the Governor of The Grand Canyon State. But of less interest to the rest of the country right then. The world wanted a decision on Obamacare. And somehow the immigration ruling seemed to pale into insignificance next to it on this particular day.

Now it would be another three days of waiting. The media didn't waste the time. Every news outlet continued to be filled with stories. President Obama and the Democrats waited out the dwindling hours with steely determination. But their bravado could no longer hide their growing concern. The *New York Times* said it best.

"But even if the White House is a fortress of message discipline, it cannot disguise the potential heartbreak for Mr. Obama, who managed to achieve a decades-old Democratic dream despite long odds and at a steep cost."

June 28.

The last possible day for the decision to issue had finally arrived. At this point, the steps of the Supreme Court looked more like a wartime demonstration than a sunny summer day of peace. The Congressional halls had taken on somewhat of a carnival atmosphere. There were no somber discussions of settlements—one was no longer possible. Just two polarized groups, each certain of the accuracy of its own polarized opinion.

It finally arrived.

I had the TV on CNN and my laptop fired up to the SCOTUS blog—the minute-by-minute coverage of the Supreme Court of the United States. CNN at first reported that the individual mandate had been struck down.

I watched as Amy Howe typed in her blog entry correcting the CNN story.

Confusion continued.

Her summary put it this way:

"The Affordable Care Act, including its individual mandate that virtually all Americans buy health insurance, is constitutional. There were not five votes to uphold it on the ground that Congress could use its power to regulate commerce between the states to require everyone to buy health insurance. However, five Justices agreed that the penalty that someone must pay if he refuses to buy insurance is a kind of tax that Congress can impose using its taxing power. That is all that matters. Because the mandate survives, the Court did not need to decide what other parts of the statute were constitutional, except for a provision that required states to comply with new eligibility requirements for Medicaid or risk losing their funding. On that question, the Court held that the provision is constitutional as long as states would only lose new funds if they didn't comply with the new requirements, rather than all of their funding."

At the end of the day, Obamacare brought the Lipitor saga full circle for me. The Food and Drug Administration would now be allowed to approve more generic drugs—the very thing I had fought hard to stop for so many years. I sighed at the irony of it all. How had it come to this? How was it possible that one of the once most profitable industries in the United States was now fighting for survival? I thought of General Cornwallis's words as he surrendered his sword to end the Revolutionary War.

"Everything will change; everything has changed."

CHAPTER 30 - SHARP EDGES
New York City, November–December 2012

In November, another pharmaceutical story in the news closed the chapter on the first Lipitor battle. The *New York Times* was among a dozen news sources to carry it.

"Ranbaxy Pharmaceuticals has recalled dozens of lots of its generic version of the cholesterol drug Lipitor because some may contain tiny glass particles. It was the latest in a string of manufacturing deficiencies that once led American regulators to bar imports of the Indian company's medicines. Ranbaxy is operating under increased scrutiny from the Food and Drug Administration because of quality lapses at multiple Ranbaxy factories over the last several years."

The following week, on November 30 of all possible dates, Ranbaxy announced they were stopping production of Lipitor altogether. Again, the *New York Times* carried the story.

"Ranbaxy Pharmaceuticals, the largest producer of the generic version of Lipitor, has halted production of the drug until it can figure out why glass particles may have ended up in pills that were distributed to the public, the Food and Drug Administration announced Thursday."

The irony was laughable, the reality pathetic. The FDA makes the research-based companies jump through multiple hoops before granting health approvals for its drugs, but, in the clamor to get cheaper generics to the market, they'd allowed a product with glass particles in it to reach consumers. To add to the irony, after a ten-year battle to get its generic product to market, Ranbaxy now, just one year later, had to pull its Lipitor drug off the market. The third November 30 date completed the trilogy of events: Peter's retirement, Lipitor's loss of exclusivity, and now Ranbaxy's loss of the coveted first generic filer position they had fought for almost a decade to protect. I felt sorry for Jay, who had worked so hard to procure it.

* * *

I, meanwhile, continued to struggle. I had opened a restaurant, started writing this book, opened my own law firm, and yet I'd not been able to regain my full emotional bearings. To my surprise, despite his earlier frustration with my commitment to a job that was all too literally sickening me, my husband encouraged me to forget about the past. Our initial conversations on the subject were short and tense.

"Traci, let the past go. Set yourself free."

I knew he was right.

Despite the fact that the pending Lipitor antitrust case entered a "sleepy" stage of litigation as both sides battled over motions to amend complaints and likewise dismiss them, December did not hold much holiday cheer for Big Pharma. The United States Supreme Court granted certiorari and agreed to hear Federal Trade Commission v. Actavis. The Court's decision marked the latest chapter in the decade-long effort by the FTC to bring before the Court the issue of pay-for-delay provisions in patent settlements. Although the Lipitor settlement included no such provision, the plaintiffs in the antitrust cases alleged that it did. All eyes were now on the Supreme Court again to finally decide the legality of them.

One week before Christmas, a *Wall Street Journal* reporter, Jonathan Rockoff, came to our office to talk about our views on pay-for-delay provisions. Coincidentally, his very first news story had covered this same issue, and he had been following it for years. Even more coincidentally, Peter and I had recently written an op-ed piece on the subject and were trying to get it published. It was hard to garner any interest in it from the press, however. It was even harder to sustain any interest in it ourselves right then.

On December 14, Peter and I, as well as the entire country, had been devastated by the slaying of twenty-seven people in Newtown, Connecticut. Twenty of the victims were children. Big Pharma issues had dwindled in significance as we sought to explain what could have led a local, twenty-year-old man to break into an elementary school with an assault weapon and open fire on a roomful of innocent first graders.

CHAPTER 31 - A SUPREME MESS
New York City, March–June, 2013

The oral hearing of FTC v. Actavis at the Supreme Court was scheduled for March 25, 2013. Weeks before that date, the arguments regarding what was now referred to as the pay-for-delay case, which had made strange bedfellows of research-based companies and the generics, had captured the attention of the press.

Brett Norman opened his March 12 story for *Politico* with the arresting observation that: "Brand and generic drug companies are usually at each other's throats."

Unusually, in this case—and, in my experience, about the only case—the combatants stood in alliance against the FTC which viewed pay-for-delay clauses in patent settlements as per se anticompetitive, whereas both the research-based and generic industries maintained that they were valuable (and legal) tools for resolving patent litigation.

Paul Bisaro, CEO of Actavis, declared the FTC's characterization of these agreements to be "offensive on many levels," adding that "the settlements have brought a large number of generics to market early, saving billions." Ralph Neas, President and CEO of the Generic Pharmaceutical Association, agreed, claiming that such provisions are a "win-win."

The op-ed Peter and I had written was published in *Pharmaceutical Executive* on March 25, the day of the Supreme Court hearing. To my knowledge, "The Wrong End of the Telescope," as we'd titled the op-ed piece (our first), came at the issue from an altogether different angle, in that we did not support the position taken either by the drug companies or by the FTC. Rather, we believed that pay-for-delay provisions, while not intrinsically anticompetitive, were inherently harmful to almost everyone—to Big Pharma, to the industry's workers, to the American consumer—except the generic companies and the law firms representing them. Pay-for-delay deals encourage generics to take a chance at breaking an innovator's patent. If it can win, great. If not, maybe the owner of the patent will pay a handsome sum to induce the generic company to settle.

Speculation as to how the Supreme Court would rule on the issue abounded for several weeks but then receded. By Memorial Day, however, the story was again heating up as the anticipated Supreme Court decision drew near.

The long-awaited Supreme Court ruling arrived on June 17. The Court decided FTC v. Actavis with a 5-3 vote with one justice abstaining. As expected, the court punted to the default position by holding that the "rule of reason" should govern the lower court's assessment of pay-for-delay provisions but not defining what this rule was or how it should be applied in practice. Peter and I were concerned. Our reservations were published in our second op-ed, "FTC v. Actavis: The Rule of 'No' Reason." To our amazement, the op-ed worked its way up to the top of the leader board on the online Google News.

In its take on the decision, CNBC led with a headline that said it all:

"High Court's Generic Drug Ruling 'a Holy Mess.'"

The article pointed out the ambiguity of the Court's decision, which would leave pharmaceutical companies, as well as generics, uncertain of the financial benefits and likewise the risks in pay-for-delay deals. Analyst Ronny Gal was quoted as saying, "I think they're going to create a holy mess out of this."

We agreed with Gal's position but stated it a little less bluntly in our second op-ed.

"The majority opinion reaches an outcome that is in accord with our view that pay-for-delay provisions in patent settlements are not in the best interests of the research-based industry. However, we find the court's reasoning partially flawed and the guidelines for assessing the legality of these provisions problematic. Ironically, the dissenting opinion is virtually flawless in its reasoning and appears to understand the current 'real world' situation well, but nevertheless reaches an outcome that would perpetuate the imbalance that has led to the existence of these pay-for-delay provisions in the first place.

The first reason cited by the majority opinion is 'the specific restraint at issue has the potential for genuine adverse effects on competition.' Ironically, in practice, the opposite is true. Pay-for-delay provisions in patent settlements foster, and indeed encourage, a plethora of weak, and in some cases, meritless patent challenges. Generic companies understand that the mere filing of a patent challenge might very well produce a nice settlement reward. A sort of heads, I win, tails, you lose scenario. Either the generic wins the patent litigation or the innovator pays it a hefty sum to drop its challenge."

But the most insidious problem, in our opinion, was the effect the current H-W system had on pharmaceutical research.

"The result of this is that precious dollars that could have been used by Big Pharma to find cures for devastating diseases, including cancer, have been diverted and spent defending patent challenges instead. Worse yet, many companies have paid large sums of money to foreign generic companies, resulting in loss of American jobs, in order to protect its intellectual property from the 'what if' factor in litigation."

The Supreme Court decision brought the In Re Lipitor Antitrust Case into full focus for me once again. How would Judge Sheridan apply it to the Lipitor case?

Another moment of truth had arrived. I took a long, hard look at myself in the mirror.

I asked myself the sixty-four-dollar question again:

"Have you let the past go?"

Peter and I were still unnerved by having been followed through the streets of New York by the strange woman in the psychedelic pants in March. And I was about to be injured again.

One week after the Supreme Court decision, while descending the marble staircase at Grand Central, I tripped and fell down the last few steps. Breaking bones in both feet, spraining my right wrist and ankle, and ripping my hip labrum, I'd known before I hit the bottom that I'd be back at the physical therapy center again. Dread overwhelmed me— not so much because of the pain I knew I would endure, but more for the pain I would have to witness in others. A PT center is very much a battlefield all its own.

My rapid descent left me, needless to say, in wretched shape. As much as this further damage to my already scarred body and psyche unnerved me, it also afforded me plenty of time, flat on my back, to review the steps I'd taken and deals I'd made in mapping out my own personal destiny.

I did not always like what I saw.

However I might try to put the past behind me, I still harbored, perhaps not without reason, a grudge. At whom, I was not sure. I was not alone in my resentment, as the sentiments expressed on many pharmaceutical blogs attested, as well as the critical newspaper stories, not to mention the *Fortune* article. But I knew, without question, that I had to get over myself. I also knew that if I looked at the nucleus of my anger in a truthful way, it was directed at myself.

* * *

As of this writing, the Lipitor antitrust case is still quiet despite the Supreme Court decision. The Pfizer/Ranbaxy settlement is complex as the article in *Patent Docs*, written by Keven Noonan, would make clear.

"This settlement agreement was highly complex, encompassing three separate ANDA litigations as well as more than two dozen other actions in foreign jurisdictions, and involving Pfizer drugs Accupril and Caduet as well as Lipitor. The Lipitor ANDA litigation involved seven patents....Ranbaxy was the first ANDA filer, and its Paragraph IV letter with regard to the '893, '995, '156, '971 and '104 patents asserted non-infringement based on its ANDA for sale of amorphous (not crystalline) Lipitor."

But for the time being, both parties wrangle over motions to dismiss, motions to add new causes of action, adequacy of pleadings, and various other less-than-interesting preliminary issues. If the case ever does get going, I will bear witness to the truth. Not because I owe it to Pfizer. Because I owe it to myself. Because I owe it to justice.

* * *

It has been difficult for me to tell this story. I had carefully concealed, even from myself, the pain of my broken relationship with my mother. A false bravado told the world I was fine, that the past had not affected me. All was forgotten.

But the past, however, is not just what I need to forget but what I also need to forgive. Starting with myself. For all the hurtful things I have done and left undone, for all the hurtful things I have said. For the thoughts and intentions I have had over the years that have not always been loving, and even for the resentment, and indeed at times hatred, I have harbored for the very woman, Jean Alice Tully, who gave me life.

And especially for what I did that fateful summer day, and the secret I had buried in my heart until now. When the shattered nerves of the twelve-year old girl I once was could no longer witness my little brother being whipped, and with white-knuckled clenched fists I had pounced on my mother, I'd known, even at twelve years old, that I had provoked not only that whipping, but many of the others as well. I'd known that my mother's frayed nerves were shot. I'd known that my mother suffered from chronic back pain brought on by the shattered vertebra in her lower back that erupted at the moment she delivered her first child, Traci Jean Medford, into the world. Yet despite my mother's repeated requests to stop "roughhousing," angry that I could not get her attention any other way, I would persist until she eventually, inevitably, exploded. I am not seeking to justify or excuse my mother's actions, rather to simply own the part of this story that is my responsibility.

Triumphing over fear with courage and allowing love to rule the heart—Nelson Mandela's words and actions when faced with the choice between love and hate stare me in the face. When life had afforded him this decision, he chose love because he figured it would do a better job.

For me, now, after all the blame and punishments have been meted out, for others, as well as for myself, that is the only choice I have left.

Hate is far too difficult a burden to bear.

Love is the only path I believe will lead me out of this darkness.

"As I walked out the door toward the gate that would lead to my freedom, I knew that if I didn't leave my bitterness and hatred behind, I'd still be in prison."
—Nelson Mandela

EPILOGUE
Mahopac, New York, June 6, 2015

I grab my morning coffee. With it and the *New York Times*, I settle into my chair. A light morning mist hangs over the lake outside our window. I can hear the ducks quacking at the end of the dock. It is my 60th birthday.

Joel and I had purchased this lakeside retreat just a short hour's drive north of New York City and only five minutes from the restaurant. Kyra is already here. Chad will arrive by train later in the morning.

Today, I feel at peace.

It has been a hard-fought victory. For the last two years, I have struggled with doubts and self-recriminations. I have replayed every move that has led me to this day. No amount of prayer or therapy freed me from my suffering.

But one day I picked up a copy of Pam Grout's *E-Squared* and did the coat hanger experiment described in it. The first time I saw those two rods move with nothing more than the power of my thoughts, I knew in that instant that all those old sayings about the power of positive thinking had some basis in scientific truth. I couldn't wait to show the experiment to Peter and get him to try it. He had the same result, and I vividly remember the look of shock on his face. He is, after all, first and foremost, a scientist.

At about the same time, I was introduced to a collection of channeled messages called *The Pathwork*. Those recorded lectures confirmed what I saw with the coat hanger experiment. My thoughts do act like energy currents. They control my emotions which in turn control my life. Hence, if I can control my thoughts, I can control my life. This is not easy to do, but as with most things, it gets easier with practice.

So today, I am finally free. Free of the pain of my childhood, free of my Pfizer history, free of my own inner demons, self-created and otherwise.

My attention is wandering between the headlines in the *Times* and the rather comforting quacks of ducks when Kyra calls to me from my bathroom. She'd been rummaging through my cabinet in search of something or other she'd forgotten to pack.

"Mom, come here please."

Her voice has that pointed tone of disapproval she uses when I've done something, in her eyes, to warrant it. With a sigh of resignation, I put down the newspaper and push myself up from the chair.

"What's up?"

"This! That's what. What is it?" she demands, holding up my jar of face cream. She turns it around and starts reading the label.

"It's a face cream," I reply with a shrug.

"It's a face cream for old ladies!" she exclaims.

"Yeah, I guess it is."

I quickly back out of the bathroom and head down the hall.

"Mom!"

I stop and turn around. Kyra is peeking around the bathroom door and shaking her head.

"I never thought I'd see the day that you would buy a wrinkle cream."

* * *

Driving to the station to pick up Chad, I replay the exchange in my head. Was Kyra genuinely upset about a face cream? That I did indeed have wrinkles? Or was it something more fundamental, like the fact that I had aged so noticeably over the past few years, and in that aging, she could see the evidence of the inevitable?

Whatever, today it is summer, and I am alive. Despite it all.

As I'd dressed that morning, I'd run my hand over my shoulders, over my scars: the scars on the shoulders I'd worn out those mornings five years ago when I'd pound out my stress—harder, faster—in the water before heading off to another day on the pharmaceutical industry's battlefield.

Dr. Howard's repair of both my rotator cuffs had left four tiny scars on each shoulder, and one long, ugly one down my right arm where my bicep tendon had been reattached. But the scars did not bother me—not even the long, ugly one.

Those scars attested to the fact that I was alive.

For what I had survived, I could no doubt have justified anger—anger that the Lipitor settlement agreement was being attacked; anger that I'd had to endure two rotator cuff surgeries; anger at my mother; anger at myself for not having played the corporate game better. But anger requires energy and then wastes it. And I have no energy to spare, let alone waste, in my quest for something beyond indignation, righteous or not. Something beyond rulings, judgments, penalties, and costs—something like grace.

I put down the newspaper and head out to see what Joel is making in his shop. He doesn't see me enter; he is engrossed in his latest wood carving project. In that instant I realize that he has suffered far more than I have as a result of my commitment to the job. I had justified all the business trips, long days at the office, and missed dinners by saying to myself that I was providing a good life for my family.

But today as I watch Joel carve, I realize that I had it all wrong, and that Kyra always knew that. Because to love is to fiddle back, finger joint, gouge, grain, and finally, with a fair measure of grace, to hinge back together.

That is what my family has done.

As much as I have trusted my instincts, my gut, in making crucial decisions throughout my life, I have always and equally relied upon my mind to focus and define them and then to implement them to optimum effect. My twelve-year-old self had calculated the odds that the referee might not have seen my false start in that relay race, and the attorney in me has spent years collecting, culling, sorting and linking together the pieces of intricate legal puzzles until they were solved.

Yet, my mind has never, ever been able to lead me to a place of grace or forgiveness.

For that journey, I have had to rely on my heart.

Author's Final Note to Readers

At a recent wedding, a woman approached me and asked if she could asked me a question about pharmaceuticals. I had thought she wanted to ask me about a medicine.

But no.

She wanted to tell me her story—how she'd one day detected, and at the same time tried to deny, the first signs of an impending health horror; how she was suffering the effects of Lou Gehrig's disease, also known as ALS (amyotrophic lateral sclerosis). She concluded with a factual, dispassionate account of the eventuality that would be her death—when she would lose the ability to breathe.

I had thought that she was going to ask me about the legalities of assisted suicide. She didn't. She asked me a simple, if unsettling question instead:

"Why have the pharmaceutical companies stopped looking for a cure for ALS?"

I could have told her the truth—that the cost of discovering a new drug and getting it to market is a billion dollars, and so the research dollars must be spent on diseases that affect large populations. I could have reminded her of a fact that she already knew too well—that very few people, fortunately, get ALS, and, therefore, the amount of money that could be expected to be earned from finding a cure for it might be small. The occasion—a wedding celebrating the beginning of a happy couple's new life together—did not encourage a matter-of-fact recital of practical business considerations, and I was pretty sure that, in any event, she would not have been interested in industrial realities. All that mattered to her at that moment was that no cure for ALS lay on the pharmaceutical horizon, and, for her, that was a fatal matter of fact.

In our efforts to bring affordable medicines to the American people, we have helped to cripple the very industry that invents the drugs in the first place. Many people have written about Big Pharma's woes, but none with quite the insight as Alex Kandybin and Vessela Genova in their February 28, 2012 article.

"But the era of the blockbuster drug is nearing an end. In the U.S. alone, branded pharmaceuticals accounting for some US$120 billion in annual revenues (including Lipitor, Zyprexa, Plavix, and Seroquel) will be coming off patent in the next few years, opening the way to generics and eroding a major source of the industry's profits. To be sure, there is still plenty of room for improvement in the medications people take, and no shortage of human suffering to alleviate. But it is doubtful whether big pharmaceutical companies will be able to pursue these goals within the old model of developing exclusive new pills that they can sell under patent protection. For one thing, pharma companies in the past were able to develop drugs for health problems that had never before been addressed.

In addition, the pharma companies are feeling pressure from every direction—from regulators setting the rules for drug effectiveness and safety, from managed care organizations and employers pushing back on prescription drug costs and reimbursement, from competitors coming to market with alternative brands or generics, and from disgruntled shareholders. Internally, the number of molecules in pharmaceutical company pipelines is shrinking, and the risk/reward ratio for research and development outlays is worsening. Overall, these trends have resulted in lower revenue, reduced profitability, and declining P/E valuation ratios for most major pharmaceutical companies.

The question, however, is more fundamental than what pharma companies will do for an encore in the post-blockbuster era. The question is whether they can survive at all in their present form."

Five years past my exit from Big Pharma, I now wonder whether society has made a good trade in its efforts to get cheaper drugs. Without future research, we cannot hope to find a cure for all forms of cancer. Neither generic companies nor our government will do that for us. In the last analysis, to find a cure for all forms of cancer, to be finally freed from its devastating clutches, as well as from other deadly diseases that do not yet have a cure, we should count only on research-based pharmaceutical companies.

COURT
DECISIONS

The following are excerpts from some of the court cases that provide further details for readers who may be interested.

EXCERPTS FROM JUDGE FARNAN'S DECISION

This action was brought by Plaintiffs, Pfizer Inc., Pfizer Ireland Pharmaceuticals, Warner-Lambert Company, Warner-Lambert Company, LLC and Warner-Lambert Export, Ltd. against Defendants, Ranbaxy Laboratories Limited and Ranbaxy Pharmaceuticals Incorporated for infringement of U.S. Patent No. 4,681,893 and U.S. Patent No. 5,273,995. The '893 and '995 patents pertain to an atorvastatin calcium pharmaceutical composition sold by Pfizer under the registered name Lipitor ®. Lipitor ® is prescribed by doctors for the treatment of elevated cholesterol and is the largest selling pharmaceutical in history. This lawsuit arises in connection with Abbreviated New Drug Application filed by Ranbaxy seeking to commercially manufacture, use and sell a drug product containing atorvastatin calcium as its active agent. Pfizer filed four Complaints against Ranbaxy alleging that Ranbaxy's proposed ANDA product infringes the '893 and '995 patents under 35 U.S.C. § 271(e)(2). These Complaints have been consolidated into this action. By its Complaints, Pfizer has asserted two patents against Ranbaxy, the '893 patent and the '995 patent. Specifically, Pfizer alleges infringement of claims 1-4, 8 and 9 of the '893 patent and claim 6 of the '995 patent.

In response to Pfizer's Complaints, Ranbaxy filed an Answer and several Counterclaims. Ranbaxy alleges that it does not infringe either the '893 or '995 patents. Ranbaxy also challenges the validity of the patent term extension granted by the PTO for the '893 patent. With regard to the '995 patent, Ranbaxy contends that the asserted claim of the '995 patent, claim 6, is invalid for double patenting, obviousness and anticipation. Ranbaxy also contends that the '995 patent is unenforceable as a result of inequitable conduct by Warner-Lambert Company before the PTO.

IV. The Validity Of The '995 Patent

B. *Whether Claim 6 of The '995 Patent Is Obvious In Light Of The '893 Patent*

1. Applicable Legal Principles
In pertinent part, 35 U.S.C. § 103 provides that a patent may not be obtained "if the differences between the subject matter sought to be patented and the prior art are such that the subject matter as a whole would have been obvious to a person having ordinary skill in the art...." 35 U.S.C. § 103. Obviousness is a question of law which is predicated upon several factual inquiries. Richardson-Vicks v. Upjohn Co., 122 F.3d 1476, 1479 (Fed.Cir.1997). Specifically, in determining whether a patent is invalid as obvious over the prior art, the trier of fact must consider (1) the scope and content of the prior art; (2) the level of ordinary skill in the art; (3) the differences between the claimed subject matter and the prior art; and (4) secondary considerations of non-obviousness, such as commercial success, long felt but unsolved need, failure of others, and acquiescence of others in the industry that the patent is valid. Graham v. John Deere Co., 383 U.S. 1, 17-18, 86 S.Ct. 684, 15 L.Ed.2d 545 (1966). The party challenging validity on the grounds of obviousness must establish that the patents are invalid by clear and convincing evidence. C.R. Bard, Inc. v. M3 Sys., 157 F.3d 1340, 1351 (Fed.Cir.1998).

2. Analysis
Ranbaxy asserts the '893 patent as the relevant prior art to be considered in the analysis of whether the '995 patent is

obvious. The '893 patent was cited and relied upon during the prosecution of the '995 patent. With respect to the level of ordinary skill in the art pertaining to the '995 patent, the parties essentially agree that one skilled in the art would have at least a Bachelor's degree in organic or medicinal chemistry, a general knowledge of statins, several years of bench work in organic molecule synthesis and some general knowledge of biochemistry and enzymology. The parties also agree that one skilled in the art would have knowledge pertaining to the stereochemistry of pharmaceutically active ingredients and the resolving of racemates. Ranbaxy asserted at trial that one skilled in the art would have a Ph.D., but Ranbaxy contends that this educational difference is immaterial to the obviousness analysis. To the extent the Court is required to make a finding on this disputed issue, the Court finds that one skilled in the art is not necessarily required to have a Ph.D. in light of the skill and knowledge base one can obtain through the work experience identified by the parties as essential to the level of ordinary skill in the relevant art.

Having identified the level of skill in the art and the relevant prior art, the Court must next consider the differences between the prior art and the claimed subject matter, as well as the objective indicia of non-obviousness. In conducting this analysis, the Court also considers whether one skilled in the art would have been motivated to modify the '893 patent to reconstruct atorvastatin calcium.

Unlike the '995 patent which is specifically directed to the calcium salt of atorvastatin, the '893 patent does not specifically name, exemplify or depict a specific calcium salt. Rather, the '893 patent broadly includes calcium among at least 50 possible salts, and mentions no preference for calcium as compared with the other possible salts. Indeed, if any salt was preferred at the time among the more than fifty to one hundred available, the evidence indicates that it would have been sodium salt. Further, the art at the time suggests that the selection of salts is a difficult task. Given the unique properties each salt imparts to the parent compound, salt selection is not a routine process and the success of a given salt is not easily predicted. In these circumstances, the Court finds that, at best, it would have been obvious for medicinal chemists to try various salts in an attempt to find a salt with properties suitable for pharmaceutical use. However, "obvious to try" does not equate with obviousness for purposes of Section 103. (Obvious to try has long been held not to constitute obviousness.) Accordingly, the Court is not persuaded that one skilled in the art would have been motivated to select calcium, or that one could have a reasonable expectation that the selection of calcium would be successful.

Ranbaxy also contends that it would have been obvious to one skilled in the art to obtain atorvastatin calcium from the racemates of atorvastatin disclosed in the '893 patent. The Court disagrees with Ranbaxy's position. Although the '893 patent identifies racemic atorvastatin lactone as compound 1, there is nothing in the '893 patent expressing a preference for that compound as opposed to the thousands of other individual compounds identified by the '893 patent. Moreover, the Court is not persuaded that one skilled in the art during the relevant time period would have selected compound 1 as a starting point for the ultimate separation of that compound into its individual enantiomers. First, the prior art indicates that the motivation at the time was to develop racemates and make structural changes to the compounds to increase their activity, not to resolve those racemates into individual isomers. The resolution of racemates into their individual isomers yielded, at best, an expectation of a two-fold increase in activity. This modest increase in activity was offset by the difficulty and complexity of the resolution process, as well as the reduced yield and increased waste disposal problems. Further, the Court is persuaded by Dr. Roush's testimony, that if there was a motivation to resolve the racemates, a medicinal chemist attempting to improve the activity of the compounds in the '893 patent would begin with the most active compound identified in the patent, compound 3. As Dr. Roush explained, expectations at the time would have led a medicinal chemist to expect no more than a two-fold increase in activity from racemic compound 1, which is the same activity level as compound 3 before compound 3 was separated into its component enantiomers. As a result, the Court cannot conclude that there was any motivation in the prior art or reasonable expectation of success that would lead one skilled in the art to resolve compound 1 into its individual enantiomers.

In addition to the differences between the prior art and claim 6 of the '995 patent and the lack of motivation to resolve compound 1 described in the '893 patent into its individual enantiomers, the Court also concludes that objective indicia of non-obviousness support the validity of claim 6 of the '995 patent. Prior to the filing date of the '995 patent, no commercial statin had been marketed in the form of a calcium salt. Lipitor ®, which contains as its active pharmaceutical agent the compound recited in claim 6 of the '995 patent, was the first such product and its commercial and medical success, though unexpected, has been well-documented. Ranbaxy contends that Lipitor ®'s success is the result of Pfizer's marketing strategies and not the efficacy of the product; however, Pfizer has produced several studies and clinical trials which demonstrate the benefits derived from the use of atorvastatin calcium and its superiority over other compounds. In the Court's view, this evidence is sufficient to demonstrate that Lipitor ®'s success was the result of its medical efficacy compared with other products.

To this effect, the Court also finds that Lipitor ® satisfied a long-felt need in the medical community to provide patients with more effective statins to help them achieve their LDL goals. Despite the efforts of others to make effective statins, Lipitor ® proved to be more successful than those products available on the market at the time. Indeed, the fact that Ranbaxy has chosen to copy Lipitor ® in its ANDA further demonstrates the success and efficacy of Lipitor ® compared with other available products.

In sum, the Court concludes that Ranbaxy has not demonstrated that claim 6 of the '995 patent is obvious in light of the '893 patent. The '893 patent claims a genus of compounds, while the '995 patent claims a species of that genus. There was no motivation in the prior art to select the species compound of atorvastatin calcium from the genus of compounds identified in the '893 patent, and absent such a motivation, the Court cannot conclude that the '893 genus patent renders the '995 species patent obvious. In addition, the Court concludes that indicia of non-obviousness support the validity of the '995 patent. Accordingly, the Court concludes that Ranbaxy has not demonstrated by clear and convincing evidence that claim 6 of the '995 patent is obvious.

V. The Enforceability Of The '995 Patent Due To Inequitable Conduct

A. *Applicable Legal Principles*
Patent applicants and their patent attorneys have a duty of candor, good faith and honesty in their dealings with the PTO. The duty of candor, good faith and honesty includes the duty to submit truthful information and the duty to disclose to the PTO information known to the patent applicants or their attorneys which is material to the examination of the patent application. Breach of the duty of candor, good faith and honesty may constitute inequitable conduct. Id. If it is established that a patent applicant engaged in inequitable

conduct before the PTO, the entire patent application so procured is rendered unenforceable.

To establish inequitable conduct due to the failure to disclose material information or the submission of false information, the party raising the issue must prove by clear and convincing evidence that (1) the information is material; (2) the knowledge of this information and its materiality is chargeable to the patent applicant; and (3) the applicant's submission of false information or its failure to disclose this information resulted from an intent to mislead the PTO. Information is deemed material if there is a substantial likelihood that a reasonable examiner would have considered the material important in deciding whether to issue the application as a patent. Accordingly, a reference does not have to be prior art to be material information that must be disclosed to the PTO. Further, "an otherwise material reference need not be disclosed if it is merely cumulative of or less material than other references already disclosed."

Intent to deceive is rarely established by direct evidence, and therefore, may be inferred from the facts and circumstances surrounding the applicant's overall conduct. In determining whether the applicant's overall conduct evidences an intent to deceive the PTO, the Federal Circuit has emphasized that the challenged "conduct must be sufficient to require a finding of deceitful intent in the light of all the circumstances." Once materiality and intent have been established, the court must conduct a balancing test to determine "whether the scales tilt to a conclusion that 'inequitable conduct' occurred." Generally, the more material the omission, the less the degree of intent that must be shown to reach a conclusion of inequitable conduct.

The question of whether inequitable conduct occurred is equitable in nature. As such, the ultimate question of whether inequitable conduct occurred is committed to the sound discretion of the trial court.

B. *Whether Warner-Lambert Engaged In Equitable Conduct During The Prosecution Of The '995 Patent*

Ranbaxy contends that, during the prosecution of the '995 patent, Warner-Lambert withheld material information concerning other patents in their portfolio and misrepresented the cholesterol inhibition activity of the compounds at issue. Specifically, Ranbaxy contends that the '080 patent filed in February 1988 and its CIP application filed in February 1989 were not disclosed to the PTO, but both of these references give rise to prima facie unpatentability of the '995 patent based on obvious-type double patenting. Ranbaxy also contends that Warner-Lambert withheld results from in vivo experiments called AICS screens ("AICS data") and results from in vitro experiments called CSI screens ("CSI data") which demonstrated no significant difference in activity of the material compounds. Ranbaxy contends that this information was contrary to the representations made by Warner-Lambert, through Dr. Roth and Dr. Daignault, that its compound had "activity at least ten-fold more than that of the racemate," and therefore, showed "surprising and unexpected results" because the activity of the R isomer would only be expected to be twice that of the racemic mixture. As a result of the failure to disclose this information, Ranbaxy contends that Warner-Lambert intentionally deceived the PTO as to the patentability of the '995 invention. In response, Pfizer contends that Ranbaxy cannot establish intent to deceive the PTO. Pfizer contends that Dr. Roth dealt with two separate attorneys for the '080 patent and the '995 patent, and that he never considered whether the '080 patent should have been brought to the attention of the '995 patent examiner, because the patents involved what Dr. Roth considered to be two very different inventions. Pfizer also contends that Dr. Daignault had limited involvement in the '995 patent prosecution and that while he signed papers for the 'o80 patent, he did not do significant substantive work on it. As a result, Pfizer contends that Dr. Daignault was not knowledgeable in the 'o80 patent, and therefore, he had no deliberate intent to withhold it from the PTO.

As for the AICS and CSI data, Pfizer contends that Ranbaxy's allegations of inequitable conduct based on the alleged withholding of data are hindsight reconstructions that fail to take into account the "real world" conditions under which Dr. Roth discovered Lipitor ®. Pfizer contends that Dr. Roth had no intent to deceive the PTO and that the data identified by Ranbaxy is not material.

1. The 'o80 patent and the CIP application for the 'o80 patent
Reviewing the record as it relates to the 'o80 patent and the CIP application for the 'o80 patent, the Court concludes that Ranbaxy has not established that Dr. Daignault or Dr. Roth intentionally deceived the PTO by failing to disclose these references. Although Dr. Daignault signed the application papers for the 'o80 patent as the attorney of record, Dr. Tinney was responsible for the substantive preparation of the application. At the time, Dr. Tinney could not sign the papers, because he had not yet passed the patent bar. Prosecution of the 'o80 patent was abandoned in favor of the expanded CIP application. The expanded CIP application, and not the original 'o80 application contains the express disclosure of enantiomers upon which Ranbaxy relies.

By the time the 'o80 CIP application was ready for filing, Dr. Tinney had his PTO registration. As a result, Dr. Tinney, prepared and prosecuted the 'o80 CIP application. Dr. Daignault had no involvement in the CIP, and Dr. Tinney and Dr. Daignault both testified that they did not discuss the 'o80 CIP application with each other.

The '995 patent application was prepared and prosecuted by a different Warner-Lambert attorney, Joan Theirstein. Dr. Tinney had no involvement in the '995 prosecution, and Dr. Tinney and Ms. Theirstein never discussed the '080 issued patent or CIP application with each other. In December 1991, Ms. Theirstein left Warner-Lambert suddenly and Dr. Daignault was required to assume the prosecution of the '995 patent on short notice. Dr. Daignault filed and argued the appeal of the anticipation rejection to the PTO Board of Appeals and signed the issue fee transmittal to the PTO in early September 1993. Dr. Daignault testified that he was not consciously aware of the '080 CIP application at the time he prosecuted the '995 appeal in December 1991, which was approximately two years after his involvement with the '080 patent. Dr. Daignault also testified that he never considered citing the '080 patent during the '995 appeal period or thereafter. Dr. Daignault was responsible for more than 150 ongoing active patent prosecutions in addition to his administrative duties at the time. Dr. Daignault's involvement with the '080 patent and the CIP application were limited and the duties he assumed with regard to the '995 patent were likewise limited in nature. In these circumstances, the Court cannot conclude that Dr. Daignault's failure to consciously consider the '080 patent or the CIP was the result of any intent to deceive the PTO.

With respect to Dr. Roth, the evidence adduced at trial demonstrates that Dr. Roth dealt with two separate attorneys during the '080 and '995 patent prosecution. Dr. Roth testified that he never considered whether the '080 patent or CIP application should have been brought to the attention of the patent examiner. In this regard, Dr. Roth testified that he considered the patents to involve two different processes. In these circumstances, the Court cannot conclude that Dr. Roth's views were based on any intent to deceive the PTO.

Accordingly, the Court is not persuaded that Dr. Roth acted intentionally to withhold the '080 patent from the PTO.

2. The AICS data

Ranbaxy contends that Dr. Roth intentionally withheld in vivo rat data generated in an AICS screen from the PTO during the prosecution of the '995 patent. This data was contained in a May 1989 research report in which the author, a biologist named Dr. Krause, concluded that the R-isomer was "approximately twofold more active at inhibiting cholesterol synthesis acutely in vivo" compared to racemic atorvastatin. DTX-11. Ranbaxy contends that this material was intentionally withheld from the PTO, because it contradicted other data provided by Warner-Lambert to support its assertion that the R-isomer was ten times more active than the racemate.

Reviewing the testimony and evidence adduced at trial in light of the applicable legal standards, the Court concludes that Ranbaxy has not demonstrated by clear and convincing evidence that the in vivo rat data was material or intentionally with-held by Dr. Roth. AICS in vivo assays are not used to measure the absolute or intrinsic inhibitory activity of a compound. Particularly, the fact that these assays are conducted in vivo, in a live animal, presents a variety of complicating factors that make these studies unreliable for determining whether a given compound is having a direct effect on the inhibition of cholesterol synthesis. Instead, in vitro data is the best and most relevant data for comparing the absolute or intrinsic activity of compounds to inhibit cholesterol biosynthesis. Accordingly, the Court cannot conclude that Ranbaxy has established, by clear and convincing evidence, that this data was material.

In addition, the Court cannot conclude that Dr. Roth intentionally withheld this data from the PTO with the intent to deceive. Dr. Roth testified that he believed in vivo data could not be used to measure the intrinsic inhibitory activity of a compound, because it was influenced by a number of factors such as metabolism and absorption in the body. Indeed, Dr. Roth did not use AICS data to make quantitative comparisons of the activity of compounds or in developing his SAR or QSAR theories which led to the discovery of atorvastatin calcium. Thus, the Court finds that the evidence demonstrates that Dr. Roth made a good faith determination that the AICS data was not relevant.

Ranbaxy argues that the AICS data was submitted to the FDA when Warner-Lambert sought approval for Lipitor ®, and therefore, it must have been material data. However, a determination of materiality before the PTO is not governed by that which is required for submission to the FDA. Ranbaxy refers the Court to the Federal Circuit's decision in Bruno Independent Living Aids, Inc. v. Acorn to support its argument that material submitted to the FDA should have been disclosed to the PTO and the failure to do so demonstrates an intent to deceive. In the Court's view, however, the Bruno case is distinguishable from the circumstances here. In Bruno, the Federal Circuit rejected the patentee's assertion that certain representations made to the FDA about prior art were only relevant to securing FDA approval and had no bearing on whether the patentee knew those references were material prior art for purposes of patentability. In reaching this conclusion, the Federal Circuit highlighted the fact that the FDA submission was prepared by the same individual who was involved in the prosecution of the patent-in-suit and that individual had asked an attorney to conduct a prior art search in preparation for the filing of the patent application. Unlike Bruno, the FDA submission in this case does not involve prior art but the submission of data, which the Court has already concluded was withheld based on the credible assertion that the data was unreliable.

Further, Dr. Roth was not involved in the FDA submissions, and therefore, the FDA submissions cannot be used to infer that Dr. Roth believed the AICS data was material to patentability. Accordingly, the Court cannot conclude that Ranbaxy has established by clear and convincing evidence that Dr. Roth intentionally withheld material data from the PTO with the intent to deceive the PTO as to the inhibitory activity of atorvastatin calcium.

3. The CSI data

Ranbaxy also contends that Warner-Lambert intentionally withheld certain CSI data and manipulated the CSI data that was disclosed to deceive the PTO and support its assertions concerning the activity of atorvastatin calcium. Ranbaxy contends that like the AICS data discussed above, the withheld CSI data showed the comparative activity between the R-isomer and the racemic compound to be far lower than the "ten times" difference asserted by Warner-Lambert. Ranbaxy contends that this data was material to patentability and not cumulative, and therefore, Warner-Lambert had a duty to disclose it.

The biological data contained in the '995 patent specification were generated from an in vitro assay called CSI. The CSI assay measures the absolute or inherent activity of compounds to inhibit cholesterol biosynthesis. The data for the sodium salt of the R-isomer and S-isomer are from the same experiment, CSI test 120, the most recent CSI experiment available to Dr. Roth at the time. The data collected for racemic atorvastatin sodium salt represents an average of five separate assays.

Ranbaxy contends that the use of this average number was misleading and demonstrates an intent to deceive the PTO. The Court concludes there was no intent to deceive. The experts agree that head-to-head testing provides the best way to compare quantitative differences in activity. Dr. Roth initially located a head-to-head comparison for the sodium salts of the R-isomer and S-isomer, but the sodium racemate was not included in that experiment. Dr. Roth did what he considered to be the next best thing, which was to collect all of the then-available data for the racemate and calculate the historical average. When asked to check for additional data, Dr. Roth then found a single head-to-head comparison with all three forms of calcium salt in CSI-118. This data was submitted to the PTO in Dr Roth's declaration. Ranbaxy also points to other data which Dr. Roth allegedly concealed, including the atorvastatin lactone value from CSI-107, the racemic sodium salt value from CSI 118 and the racemic calcium salt data from CSI 119. The Court finds that this evidence is insufficient to establish clearly and convincingly that this data was withheld to intentionally deceive the PTO. Dr. Roth has alleged credible and good faith reasons for his failure to include certain data in his reports. For example, the atorvastatin compounds tested in CSI-107 were based on Warner-Lambert's first crude attempt to resolve racemic atorvastatin. The results were impure R-trans and S-trans isomers that were contaminated with their opposite isomer. Dr. Roth did not know what effect this contamination would have on the biological activity of the R-isomer, so he relied on comparisons using pure isomers.

As for Ranbaxy's assertion that the racemic sodium value from CSI-118 should have been disclosed along with the calcium values, Dr. Roth explained that it is inappropriate to compare across salts, because different salts have different solubilities. Thus, Dr. Roth believed that it was only appropriate to compare the same salts within an experiment. Along a similar vein, Dr. Roth did not provide the data from CSI-119, because he believed it was inappropriate to compare individual data points from different experiments. CSI 119 was not a head-to-head comparison, and was not a repeat of CSI 118. Moreover, the CSI 119 experiment showed a worse than normal solubility problem noted as "chunks," a problem which was not noted in the CSI 118 experiment12, which was fully disclosed in Dr. Roth's declaration and is the only CSI experiment where all three calcium salts of racemic atorvastatin and the R-isomer and the S-isomer were tested head-to-head. In the Court's view, sound reasons support Dr. Roth's decision not to submit certain CSI data to the PTO, and therefore, the Court cannot conclude that Ranbaxy has demonstrated that Dr. Roth intended to deceive the PTO by withholding certain CSI data.

4. Summary

In sum, the Court concludes that Ranbaxy has not established by clear and convincing evidence that the '995 patent was procured through inequitable conduct. Although the '080 patent was not revealed during the prosecution of the '995 patent, the Court is not persuaded that it was intentionally withheld. The circumstances related to the drafting and prosecution of the '080 and '995 patents, including the workload of Dr. Daignault and his limited roles in each of the patents, suggest that Dr. Daignault was not dishonest in his claim that he did not consider the '080 patent during the prosecution of the '995 patent. Similarly, the Court cannot conclude that Dr. Roth was dishonest in his view that the '080 patent and '995 patents referred to two separate inventions.

As for the data submission issue, the Court is not persuaded that Warner-Lambert manipulated or "cherry picked" data with deceitful motives to achieve a deceitful result. Pfizer had ample data to support the claims it made to the PTO, and it provided the PTO with the data it believed was scientifically sound. The Court is not persuaded that the instances of non-disclosure cited by Ranbaxy are sufficient to demonstrate an intent to deceive the PTO. Pfizer has advanced reasonable and credible grounds for the non-production of certain data that weigh against a conclusion that Warner-Lambert scientists and employees were intentionally deceiving the

PTO. Because Ranbaxy has not met its burden of establishing inequitable conduct, the Court will enter judgment in favor of Pfizer and against Ranbaxy on Ranbaxy's counterclaim that the '995 patent is unenforceable as a result of inequitable conduct.

CONCLUSION

For the reasons discussed, the Court concludes that Pfizer has established that Ranbaxy's ANDA product literally infringes the '893 and '995 patents, and therefore, the Court will enter judgment in favor of Pfizer and against Ranbaxy on Pfizer's claims of infringement. In addition, the Court concludes that Ranbaxy has not established that the '893 patent is invalid under 35 U.S.C. § 112, ¶ 1, or that the patent term extension of the '893 patent is invalid, and therefore, the Court will enter judgment in favor of Pfizer and against Ranbaxy on Ranbaxy's counterclaims of invalidity of the '893 patent and invalidity of the patent term extension. With respect to the '995 patent, the Court further concludes that Ranbaxy has not established unenforceability as a result of inequitable conduct or invalidity based on double patenting, obviousness and anticipation, and therefore, the Court will enter judgment in favor of Pfizer and against Ranbaxy on Ranbaxy's counter claims of invalidity and unenforceability of the '995 patent.

EXCERPTS FROM THE CAFC DECISION

DECIDED: August 2, 2006 Before MICHEL, Chief Judge, SCHALL and DYK, Circuit Judges. MICHEL, Chief Judge.

In this patent case concerning the prescription drug Lipitor®, which is used to reduce low-density lipoprotein (LDL) cholesterol levels, defendants-appellants Ranbaxy Laboratories Limited and Ranbaxy Pharmaceuticals, Inc. (collectively "Ranbaxy") appeal from a final judgment of the United States District Court for the District of Delaware. Plaintiffs-appellees Pfizer Inc., Pfizer Ireland Pharmaceuticals, Warner-Lambert Co., Warner-Lambert Co. LLC, and Warner-Lambert Export, Ltd. (collectively "Pfizer") filed four complaints, later consolidated into a single action...alleging that the product described in Ranbaxy's Abbreviated New Drug Application infringed United States Patent Nos. 4,681,893 and 5,273,995 under 35 U.S.C. § 271(e)(2). Ranbaxy appeals the following rulings by the district court: (1) that claim 1 of the '893 patent was infringed; (2) that the '893 patent term extension was not proven invalid; (3) that claim 6 of the '995 patent was infringed; (4) that claim 6 was not proven invalid for failure to comply with § 112, ¶ 4; as anticipated or obvious; or for non-statutory double patenting; and (5) that the '995 patent was not proven unenforceable due to inequitable conduct.

Because we agree with the district court's claim construction of claim 1 of the '893 patent, we affirm the finding of infringement. We also affirm the ruling that the '893 patent term extension was not invalid. With respect to the '995 patent, however, we reverse on the question of invalidity under § 112, ¶ 4 and find the other issues moot.

II. DISCUSSION

B. '995 Patent.

With respect to the '995 patent, numerous issues have been raised on appeal. Rather than considering them in the order presented by the appellants, we first direct our attention to the question of validity under 35 U.S.C. § 112, ¶ 4, which provides:

Subject to the following paragraph [concerning multiple dependent claims], a claim in dependent form shall contain a reference to a claim previously set forth and then specify a further limitation of the subject matter claimed. A claim in dependent form shall be construed to incorporate by reference all the limitations of the claim to which it refers.

As described above, Pfizer only asserted dependent claim 6 of the '995 patent. This claim reads: "The hemicalcium salt of the compound of claim 2." Claim 2, in turn, is dependent on claim 1, which recites the following compounds: (1) atorvastatin acid; or (2) atorvastatin lactone; or (3) pharmaceutically acceptable salts thereof. Claim 2 itself, however, only recites atorvastatin acid. Notably, it does not include the pharmaceutically acceptable salts of atorvastatin acid. Ranbaxy asserts that the district court erred in refusing to invalidate claim 6, even though it does not "incorporate by reference all the limitations of the claim to which it refers" and "then specify a further limitation of the subject matter," as required by § 112, ¶ 4. In other words, claim 6 does not narrow the scope of claim 2; instead, the two claims deal with non-overlapping subject matter.

...It is true that at the time the district court wrote its opinion, there was no applicable Federal Circuit precedent. More recently, however, we have suggested that a violation of § 112, ¶ 4 renders a patent invalid just as violations of other paragraphs of § 112 would. In Curtiss-Wright, the issue was one of claim differentiation. The court reasoned that "reading an additional limitation from a dependent claim into an independent claim would not only make that additional limitation superfluous, it might render the dependent claim invalid" for failing to add a limitation to those recited in the independent claim, as required by 35 U.S.C. § 112, ¶ 4. Indeed, "[i]nvalidity of the patent or any claim in suit for failure to comply with any requirement of sections 112 or 251 of this title "is expressly included among the available defenses to an infringement suit." 35 U.S.C. § 282(3).

We recognize that the patentee was attempting to claim what might otherwise have been patentable subject matter. Indeed, claim 6 could have been properly drafted either as dependent from claim 1 or as an independent claim—i.e., "the hemicalcium salt of atorvastatin acid."...

In light of this holding, appellants' remaining arguments concerning the '995 patent are rendered moot. We therefore decline to reach the remaining issues raised.

III. CONCLUSION

For the aforementioned reasons, we affirm-in-part, reverse-in-part and remand so the district court can modify the permanent injunction in a manner consistent with this opinion.

EXCERPTS FROM CANADIAN APPELLATE DECISION
INTRODUCTION

This is an appeal from an Order of von Finckenstein J. of the Federal Court dated January 25, 2007, dismissing the application of Pfizer Canada Inc. and Warner-Lambert Company, LLC made pursuant to section 6 of the Patented Medicines (Notice of Compliance) Regulations for an Order prohibiting the Minister of Health from issuing a Notice of Compliance (.NOC.) to Ranbaxy Laboratories Limited (.Ranbaxy.)

CSI Data

The 546 patent refers to a single set of CSI data to support the claim of increased activity for atorvastatin in comparison to the racemate. The Applications Judge was of the view that the data could not be relied upon to support a claim of ten-fold increase in inhibition for two reasons. First, the data refers to the sodium salt of atorvastatin and not the calcium salt. It is therefore not possible to draw conclusions from one salt to another. Second, the alleged ten-fold increase is based on an averaging of data for the racemic salt collected across five different experiments. The averaging of CSI results for the atorvastatin racemate does not provide a scientifically meaningful result. Before the Applications Judge, Pfizer presented the results from the CSI 118 assay, which compares the calcium salt of atorvastatin to the racemic salt of atorvastatin. The Applications Judge found that the data could not be relied upon because the test compound was not completely dissolved in the stock solution. Without knowing the concentration of the test compound in the solution, it was not possible to quantify the results of the assay.

2. AICS Data

Although the AICS data was not referred to in the 546 patent to support an increase in activity for atorvastatin, the applications judge nevertheless considered the data. It was a head-to head comparison of the racemic calcium salt of atorvastatin against the calcium salt of atorvastatin. According to the Applications Judge, the AICS data was a reliable indicator of the inherent ability of atorvastatin calcium or its racemate to inhibit cholesterol synthesis. The data revealed an increase in activity for the calcium salt of atorvastatin that was only slightly more than two-fold that of the racemic salt of atorvastatin.

According to the Applications Judge, the data did not substantiate the promise of a ten-fold increase in activity and, as a result, he concluded that the disclosure of the 546 patent was insufficient as it failed to comply with the requirements of subsection 27(3) of the Act: While these cases undoubtedly set the bar for section 27(3) very low, Pfizer in this case has not vaulted over that low bar. In essence, the 546 Patent makes two assertions, one as to activity the other as to the preferred salt. The first assertion is that there is an unexpected and surprising inhibition of cholesterol biosynthesis because of the ten-fold increase in activity between atorvastatin calcium and the racemic calcium salt. However, from the evidence presented, this statement is incorrect. The only reliable data available, the AICS data, suggests an increase in activity barely over the expected two-fold when the racemate is resolved into its individual enantiomers. This is not anywhere close to ten-fold. I fail to see how this amounts to correctly and fully describing the invention. A patentee has an obligation to make truthful statements regarding the nature of the invention in the disclosure of the patent. Here we clearly have an assertion of a ten-fold increased activity on the face of the specification. This false suggestion of a ten-fold increase in activity cannot be backed up by the data provided. Accordingly, I find the 546 Patent to be invalid for failing to meet the requirements of s. 27(3) of the Patent Act. Before the applications judge,

Ranbaxy also claimed that the 546 patent did not identify the physical properties of atorvastatin calcium that support the claim that it is the preferred embodiment of the invention, nor was there any data to support such a claim. Having found that the assertion of a ten-fold increase in activity was not correct, the applications judge did not find it necessary to test the assertion that the calcium salt of atorvastatin was the preferred embodiment of the invention. As the Applications Judge found that Pfizer did not prove that the allegation of insufficiency was unjustified, he did not consider the other allegations of invalidity raised by Ranbaxy in its NOA.

Errors of the Applications Judge

In my view, the Applications Judge erred in two respects. First, he erred in construing the 546 patent as promising a ten-fold increase in activity for atorvastatin as compared to its racemate. Second, he erred in focusing his subsection 27(3) analysis on whether the data substantiates the promise made by the patent.

Construction of the patent:
The decision in American Cyanamid v. Ethicon Limited stands for the proposition that although a patentee is not obligated to promise a result in the patent, if he does make such a promise, he will be held to it.

The Applications Judge was incorrect in construing the 546 patent as promising a ten-fold increase in activity for atorvastatin as opposed to the racemate. Rather, the promise is that the compounds covered have an unexpected and surprising inhibition of biosynthesis of cholesterol, i.e. greater than twofold although the 546 patent goes on to Page: 24 refer to CSI data set out in a table in support of this promise, in my opinion, the data is merely illustrative of the magnitude of this promise in vitro. Because a patent is notionally addressed to a person skilled in the art, its claims must be construed purposively, through the eyes of a person skilled in the art: see Whirlpool, supra, at paragraph 49; and Consolboard, supra, at 521. A person skilled in the art will be interested in whether the compounds claimed by the 546 patent have increased activity in vivo. They will know that CSI data, which represents the activity of a compound in vitro, does not reflect the activity of the compound in vivo. They will not read the patent as promising the exact increase in activity that is set out in the CSI data table. I cannot accept Ranbaxy's argument that the patentee intended the data set out in the patent to promise a ten-fold increase in inhibiting the biosynthesis of cholesterol in humans, not just in a test tube.

Subsection 27(3) analysis:
The Applications Judge was wrong in interpreting the disclosure requirement of subsection 27(3) of the Act as requiring that a patentee back up his invention by data. By so doing, he confused the requirements that an invention be new, useful and non-obvious with the requirement under subsection 27(3) that the specification disclose the use to which the inventor conceived the invention could be put. Whether or not a patentee has obtained enough data to substantiate its invention is, in my view, an irrelevant consideration with respect to the application of subsection 27(3). An analysis thereunder is concerned with the sufficiency of the disclosure, not the sufficiency of the data underlying the invention. Allowing Ranbaxy to attack the utility, novelty and/or obviousness of the 546 patent through the disclosure requirement unduly broadens the scope of an inventor's obligation under subsection 27(3) and disregards the purpose of this provision. While it is true that subsection 27(3) requires that an inventor correctly and fully describe his invention, this provision is concerned with ensuring that the patentee provide the information needed by the person

skilled in the art to use the invention as successfully as the patentee. The Supreme Court of Canada cited with approval the following passage: It is sufficient if the specification correctly and fully describes the invention and its operation or use as contemplated by the inventor, so that the public, meaning thereby persons skilled in the art, may be able, with only the specification, to use the invention as successfully as the inventor could himself. The requirement that the specification of a patent be truthful and not be misleading is not covered by subsection 27(3), but rather by subsection 53(1) of the Act. Only two questions are relevant for the purpose of subsection 27(3) of the Act. What is the invention? How does it work? In the case of selection patents, answering the question What is the invention? involves disclosing the advantages conferred by the selection. If the patent specification (disclosure and claims) answers these questions, the inventor has held his part of the bargain. In the case at bar, the 546 patent answers each of these questions. The invention consists of having identified an enantiomer, and in particular the calcium salt of that enantiomer, that is better at inhibiting the biosynthesis of cholesterol than would be expected, given the common knowledge and prior art at the time of application for the patent. How does it work? The 546 patent sets out the methods for producing the compounds covered by the patent. I also conclude that the fact that the 546 patent does not provide a justification as to why the calcium salt of atorvastatin is the preferred embodiment of the invention does not render the disclosure insufficient. As I have already indicated, there is no requirement that a patentee explain in the disclosure why and how his invention is useful. When read as a whole, a skilled reader would understand the patent as claiming that the calcium salt of atorvastatin is the compound covered by the 546 patent that demonstrates the most surprising and unexpected inhibition of cholesterol biosynthesis because it has the most preferred physical properties. Pfizer was not required to include in the

546 patent data which supports its statement that the calcium salt of atorvastatin is the preferred embodiment of the invention, nor was it required to explain why the calcium salt was the preferred embodiment.

Conclusion on disclosure under subsection 27(3)
The applications judge erred in construing the promise of the patent and mischaracterized the disclosure requirement under subsection 27(3) of the Act by asking whether there was sufficient data to substantiate the promise of the patent. Such an examination exceeds the scope of the provision. An attack on a selection patent on the basis that there is no data to support the claimed advantage is certainly relevant for the purposes of validity (most likely to the question of utility), but it is not relevant with respect to disclosure under subsection 27(3) of the Act. [64] The patent must disclose the invention and how it is made. The 546 patent does this. It also discloses the advantages that underlie the selection. This, in my view, is the extent of the requirement under subsection 27(3) of the Act, the purpose of which is to allow a person skilled in the art to make full use of the invention without having to display inventive ingenuity.

Are the allegations of obviousness, double patenting and anticipation justified?

I now turn to Ranbaxy's allegations of obviousness, double patenting and anticipation. Because of his conclusion in regard to the subsection 27(3) issue, the Judge made no findings as to whether Ranbaxy's allegations under these headings were justified. In its NOA, Ranbaxy alleges that the 546 patent is invalid for obviousness, double patenting and anticipation. Pfizer counters these allegations by saying that because the 546 patent is a selection patent, its validity depends solely on it having unexpected advantages over the class from which it is selected. In Novopharm, above, von

Finckenstein J. examined the allegations of invalidity for obviousness, double patenting and anticipation with respect to the 546 patent and found that they were not justified. This conclusion was based on his finding that the 546 patent was, on its face, a valid selection patent claiming a tenfold advantage of atorvastatin over the racemate. In his view, the fact that the 546 patent was a valid selection provided a complete answer to the allegations of invalidity (see paragraphs 56 and 96 of his Reasons). In so concluding, the Judge emphasized the fact that Novopharm's allegations of invalidity based on anticipation, obviousness and double patenting did not challenge the 546 patent on the ground that it was not a valid selection, nor did they challenge its utility. In the present matter, Ranbaxy challenges the validity of the 546 patent on the basis of obviousness, double patenting and anticipation, but it does not, under those headings, attack the sufficiency of the data that underlies the invention claimed in the 546 patent. I therefore reach the same conclusion reached by von Finkenstein J. in Novopharm, above, i.e. that the NOA does not constitute a sufficient basis upon which to challenge the data underlying the 546 patent.

On its face, the 546 patent is a selection patent, the validity of which depends on it having unexpected advantages over the class from which it is selected. By failing to attack the data underlying the selection under the headings of anticipation, obvious and double patenting, Ranbaxy has not challenged the validity of the selection. Consequently, as von Finkenstein J.A. held in Novopharm, above, there is no need to examine Ranbaxy's allegations under those headings. However, I will nonetheless say a few words regarding the issues of double patenting and anticipation.

Anticipation:
Ranbaxy submits that the 546 patent is anticipated by the 768 patent which discloses atorvastatin calcium. The NOA attacks

the novelty of the 546 patent as follows If on the construction of the 768 Patent, its claims are found to include the R(R*R*) enantiomer, then Claims 1, 2, 3, 6, 11 and 12 of the 546 Patent are invalid as lacking novelty in light of the 893 U.S. Patent (which corresponds to the 768 Patent). On that construction, the 893 Patent would disclose the R(R*R*) enantiomer and pharmaceutically acceptable salts thereof for use as a hypocholesterolemic or hypolidemic agent. All essential elements of Claims 1, 2, 3, 6, 11 and 12 of the 546 Patent would then be found in the 893 U.S. Patent. Those claims would not be novel, hence they would be invalid. Pfizer responds to this allegation in its Notice of Application, as follows: Ranbaxy also asserts that claim 6 of the 546 Patent is invalid by reason of lack of novelty in view of the 893 Patent. This assertion is without merit. Claim 6 of the 546 Patent claims subject-matter which is novel over the disclosure of the 893 Patent. Claim 6 is not anticipated by the 893 Patent. The test for anticipation was enunciated by this Court. One must, in effect, be able to look at a prior, single publication and find in it all the information which, for practical purposes, is needed to produce the claimed invention without the exercise of any inventive skill. The prior publication must contain so clear a direction that a skilled person reading and following it would in every case and without possibility of error be led to the claimed invention. In Pfizer Canada Inc. v. Canada (Minister of Health) this Court made it clear that the test for anticipation was a difficult one to meet. At paragraph 36, Malone J.A. put it as follows: This is a difficult test to meet. The Applications Judge held that a person skilled in the art would not know why to select besylate as one of the initial choices of salt, would not know whether it would form a salt of amlodipine in the solid state and would not know the particular properties of besylate or their advantage for pharmaceutical formulation. As a result of these facts, he found that a person skilled in the art would not in every case and without possibility of error be led to the claimed invention. In so doing he did not make a palpable and overriding error because there was evidence on which to base his findings. The allegation of anticipation, in my view, is not justified. A claim to a specific chemical compound cannot be anticipated by a prior art reference which only teaches a broad class of genus of compounds into which the compound falls because the prior art reference does not give directions which inevitably result in the specific compound. Ranbaxy did not allege that the prior art teaches that the calcium salt of atorvastatin would have greater inhibition activity than expected, i.e. more than two-fold.

CONCLUSION

For these reasons, I would allow the appeal, set aside the judgment of the Federal Court and, rendering the judgment which ought to have been rendered, I would prohibit the Minister from issuing a Notice under section C.08.004 of the Food and Drug Regulations to Ranbaxy for atorvastatin calcium, until after the expiry of the 546 patent. I would also allow Pfizer its costs both in the appeal and in the application.

EXCERPTS FROM U.K. APPELLATE DECISION

This appeal and cross-appeal is from a judgment of Pumfrey. He refused Ranbaxy a declaration of non-infringement of Warner-Lambert's EP (UK) 0 247 633 ("633") and held Warner-Lambert's EP (UK) 0 409 281 ("281") invalid for lack of novelty and obviousness. Each side appeals the adverse finding against it, Mr Waugh QC arguing the case for Ranbaxy and Mr Thorley QC that for Warner-Lambert. Another company, Arrow Generics, in the end by consent, joined forces with Ranbaxy. Mr Waugh appeared also for Arrow, advancing no separate case on its behalf.

Ranbaxy seek a declaration of non-infringement in respect of a particular compound. It is commonly called atorvastatin calcium. It is the optically pure [R-(R*,R*)]-2-(4-fiuorophenyl)-β,δ-dihydroxy-5-(1-methylethyl)-3-phenyl-4-[(phenylamino)-carbonyl]-lH-pyrrole-1-heptanoic acid calcium salt. The significance of "optically pure" is that the compound is an enantiomer, not a racemate. The Judge used the terminology R-(R*R*) but I will use the shorter, "R,R."

Ignoring the stereochemistry, the general structural formula of this compound admittedly falls within claim 1. It is said, however, that its stereochemistry is such as to take the product outside the claim – that the claim only covers the racemic mixture. The short issue is whether the claim is so limited or does it cover the R,R enantiomer too?

The court's first job therefore is to understand enough of the technology to be able to read the patent as it would be read by a man skilled in the art. Here there is now no dispute that such a man would have the knowledge of a medicinal chemist – someone who would be employed by a pharmaceutical company to synthesize new active ingredients. The Judge accepted the evidence of Dr Newton...

So if one has a pharmaceutical in the form of a racemate, it is highly likely that only one of the two enantiomers will provide the desired activity or most of it.   The other enantiomer will function either as an inert or near inert "filler" or even function partially to inhibit the function of the other enantiomer.   It is not suggested that the presence of the "inert" enantiomer is at all likely to enhance the function of the "active" enantiomer.

Moreover the actual drawing of formula I and of X shows what is, strictly speaking, just the R,R enantiomer. It was common ground that in practice chemists are not precise: that a figure showing a particular structure may mean, in context, a racemate The Judge held that, in the context of the patent, Formula I would have been understood to show the racemate. However, I can think of no rational reason why it should mean only the racemate in the context of this patent. It is a patent whose big idea is not about stereochemistry but about a novel substitution. The only reference to stereochemistry excludes the "cis-form" of the compounds (which would be both cis-enantiomers) but not the trans-form (which would be both trans-enantiomers). And above all the skilled reader would know that the form giving most if not all activity was the R,R form.

Mr Waugh sought to persuade us that the evidence established an unvarying convention such that, whatever the context, a figure showing a particular enantiomer denoted only that enantiomer or only the basic. Putting it another way, there is a convention that, whatever the context, such a figure could not mean both the basic and/or either enantiomer. If such a convention had been proved that would of course bear directly on the construction of the claim – for although in the end the question of construction is for the court, the court will have to go by any proved term of art or proved system of nomenclature. This is because a skilled man would read the document using such a convention.

The argument fails. The existence or otherwise of such a convention is one of fact, not law. The Judge made no such finding of fact. Indeed by his ultimate conclusion he necessarily implicitly rejected such a finding. Mr Waugh therefore had to argue that the Judge had made a wrong finding of fact – never an easy task in the Court of Appeal. He relied on certain passages in Professor Clive's evidence. He could point to no textbook setting out such a convention – which is the normal way of proving a system of nomenclature. Moreover Mr Thorley drew to our attention a number of passages in the cross-examination of Professor Clive and Dr Newton, which show that what a formula means (basic, enantiomer or either) depends entirely on context. In some contexts it will mean one or the other but not both but that is all. The Judge was not shown to be wrong.

As to Mr Waugh's point about the S,S enantiomer, even if he were right in saying that the skilled man would perceive it as having no activity whatsoever, I do not think the skilled man would read the claim as excluding the key active enantiomer. He would be much more likely to say to himself, "Well I see the claim covers the inactive form too". He might add: "I do not know why – I know how to make it, how to resolve it out of the basic, but so what?" He would not, I think, say to himself: "The patent promises that the carboxamido substitution will give surprisingly more activity, so the formula cannot include the inactive S,S and it follows it cannot also include the key active R,R compound." That would be just foolish. Such reasoning reeks of an over meticulous rather than purposive approach. It is one that flouts technical and business common sense. It may have a kind of crazy logic but it will not do.

Nor do I think that American Home Products or Pharmacia help Mr Waugh. We are, after all, concerned with the construction, and construction only, of this patent. Those were cases about validity and construction of different patents. In American Home Products the issue was whether the word "rapamycin" in the context of the patent covered not only the compound as such but any derivative of rapamycin which worked. The skilled man would, without experiment, have no idea whether any particular derivative worked. If the claim was as contended for by the patentees it would be "a starting point for a research programme" That was a reason for not giving it the wide construction contended for. There is no analogy with this case.

So even if Mr Waugh's assumption that the skilled man would perceive the S,S enantiomer to have no activity whatsoever is right, I see no reason to read the claim as limited to the basics. Of course if the assumption were wrong the whole argument would fail anyway. Mr Thorley submitted that was so – that it was never proved that the skilled man would have the perception of no activity. Mr Waugh said the Judge had so found, relying on several passages in the judgment:
I think Mr Thorley is right. The Judge did not hold that the skilled man would be sure the S,S enantiomer had no biological activity at all. That was not so for chiral compounds generally. The fact that there was no activity shown for the S,S compounds of the prior art statins made it very likely that there would also be no measurable activity for the S,S compounds of the claim. But no more. It was never actually proved that they actually have no activity or that the skilled man would be certain that was so. So this is another reason for rejecting Mr Waugh's argument – an argument which in any event was advanced rather late, not having been raised until after the cross-examination of Dr Newton.

Finally on construction I should mention the claim 3 point. This claim relates to a specific compound "having the name trans-(±) ....". The symbol ± means a basic. Each side prays claim 3 in aid as throwing light on claim 1. The Judge thought the point was neutral. So do I. One the one hand one can say that the patentee uses the symbol when he wants to denote only the basic so claim 1 must be wider. On the other because claim 1 is to a vast number of compounds, it could be that, even if all of the claim 1 class were intended to be basics, that when being much more specific about a single compound, the patentee was just being somewhat more precise.

I therefore think the Judge was right to refuse the declaration of non-infringement. It is agreed that the attack on the SPC falls with that decision.

The validity of Patent EP (UK) 0409 281

The judge held this patent anticipated by a prior earlier co-pending application WO 89/07598 and obvious over a prior published international application, EP 0247 633A. We heard Mr Thorley first on the question of anticipation. We did not need to hear Mr Waugh by way of response because we formed the view, despite Mr Thorley's admirably concise argument, that the Judge was right. In those circumstances we asked Mr Thorley whether there was any point in our hearing the obviousness appeal. He said there was none. The only way in which obviousness could become a live issue would be if our decision on anticipation were both heard and reversed by the House of Lords. Given the House's recent decision on patent novelty in Synthon's Patent, it was most unlikely that either we or it would give leave to appeal. So we decided not to hear the obviousness appeal.

To my mind this, in context, clearly teaches by way of explicit disclosure that one of the things you can make is the single enantiomer of the acid and it is that acid which can be used to make the calcium salt. In truth that way of carrying out the teaching of the earlier patent would necessarily infringe the later claim. So that claim is invalid as lacking novelty. I reject Mr Thorley's submission that one is here straying into the impermissible territory of obviousness. Alighting on atorvastatin calcium is merely picking one of the class of compounds disclosed by '598. If the claim were valid it would cover one of the alternatives explicitly taught by the citation. This is not a case of any adaptation of the prior art.

The Judge put it this way:
"[49]   It follows that the material claimed in claim 1 is an expressly specified salt (calcium) of the preferred isomer of one of the three materials explicitly specified. If one is in any doubt, it is easy to compare the final structural formula on page 12 of '281 against formula XII on page 40 of '598. They are identical, save that in '281 the calcium salt, and in '598 the acid, are shown. In fact, the synthetic route described in '598 actually produces a basic. But this time, the precise enantiomer (4R,6R) is specified. This notation means the same thing as the [R-(R*,R*   used in respect of the acid in claim 1 of '281. The evidence (which I have already discussed) was that resolution to obtain the enantiomers was common general knowledge. It is no answer to an allegation of anticipation that the specification gives clear and unmistakable directions to use the common general knowledge to produce a specific material."

That seems to me to be both elegant and clearly right.

In the result I would dismiss the appeal and cross-appeal.

EXCERPTS FROM THE SUPREME COURT DECISION

Although the anticompetitive effects of the reverse settlement agreement might fall within the scope of the exclusionary potential of Solvay's patent, this does not immunize the agreement from antitrust attack. For one thing, to refer simply to what the holder of a valid patent could do does not by itself answer the antitrust question. Here, the paragraph IV litigation put the patent's validity and preclusive scope at issue, and the parties' settlement—in which, the FTC alleges, the plaintiff agreed to pay the defendants millions to stay out of its market, even though the defendants had no monetary claim against the plaintiff—ended that litigation. That form of settlement is unusual, and there is reason for concern that such settlements tend to have significant adverse effects on competition. It would be incongruous to determine antitrust legality by measuring the settlement's anticompetitive effects solely against patent law policy, and not against procompetitive antitrust policies as well. Both are relevant in determining the scope of monopoly and antitrust immunity conferred by a patent, and the antitrust question should be answered by considering traditional antitrust factors. For another thing, this Court's precedents make clear that patent-related settlement agreements can sometimes violate the antitrust laws. Finally, the Hatch-Waxman Act's general procompetitive thrust—facilitating challenges to a patent's validity and requiring parties to a paragraph IV dispute to report settlement terms to federal antitrust regulators—suggests a view contrary to the Eleventh Circuit's. Pp. 8–14.

(b) While the Eleventh Circuit's conclusion finds some support in a general legal policy favoring the settlement of disputes, its related underlying practical concern consists of its fear that antitrust scrutiny of a reverse payment agreement would require the parties to engage in time-consuming, complex, and expensive litigation to demonstrate what would have happened to competition absent the settlement.

However, five sets of considerations lead to the conclusion that this concern should not determine the result here and that the FTC should have been given the opportunity to prove its antitrust claim. First, the specific restraint at issue has the "potential for genuine adverse effects on competition." Payment for staying out of the market keeps prices at patentee-set levels and divides the benefit between the patentee and the challenger, while the consumer loses. And two Hatch-Waxman Act features—the 180-day exclusive-right-to-sell advantage given to the first paragraph IV challenger to win FDA approval, and the roughly 30-month period that the subsequent manufacturers would be required to wait out before winning FDA approval means that a reverse settlement agreement with the first filer removes from consideration the manufacturer most likely to introduce competition quickly. Second, these anticompetitive consequences will at least sometimes prove unjustified. There may be justifications for reverse payment that are not the result of having sought or brought about anticompetitive consequences, but that does not justify dismissing the FTC's complaint without examining the potential justifications. Third, where a reverse payment threatens to work unjustified anticompetitive harm, the patentee likely has the power to bring about that harm in practice. The size of the payment from a branded drug manufacturer to a generic challenger is a strong indicator of such power. Fourth, an antitrust action is likely to prove more feasible administratively than the Eleventh Circuit believed. It is normally not necessary to litigate patent validity to answer the antitrust question. A large, unexplained reverse payment can provide a workable surrogate for a patent's weakness, all without forcing a court to conduct a detailed exploration of the patent's validity. Fifth, the fact that a large, unjustified reverse payment risks antitrust liability does not prevent litigating parties from settling their lawsuits. As in other industries, they may settle in other ways, e.g., by allowing the generic manufacturer to enter the patentee's market before the patent expires without the patentee's paying the challenger to stay out prior to that point.

(c) This Court declines to hold that reverse payment settlement agreements are presumptively unlawful. Courts reviewing such agreements should proceed by applying the "rule of reason," rather than under a "quick look" approach.

ABOUT THE AUTHOR

Traci Medford-Rosow is currently a partner in the New York City law firm, Richardson & Rosow. Previously, she enjoyed a thirty-year career at Pfizer, where she held the positions of Senior Vice President and Chief Intellectual Property Counsel, Global Head of Intellectual Property Litigation, and General Counsel of Europe. She lives in New York City and Mahopac, New York.

order at www.pegasusbooks.net